COMPLETE SINGING SCHEME FOR PRIMARY CLAS

CW00567277

Singing Express

Discovering the singer in every child

BOOK

GILLYANNE KAYES, ANA SANDERSON, JEREMY FISHER, HELEN MACGREGOR AND MAUREEN HANKE

Presented by Rosemary Amoani, Kim Chandler, Jeremy Fisher, Matthew Holmes, Nigel Pilkington, Bridgitta Roy, Kaz Simmons, Anthony Strong, Cleveland Watkiss and Matthew White

Illustrations by Christiane Engel
Design by Saffron Stocker and Jocelyn Lucas
Sound and film by Stephen Chadwick and Walk Tall Media

A&C BLACK · LONDON

contents

First published 2011 by A&C Black Publishers Ltd
36 Soho Square
London W1D 3QY
© 2011

ISBN 9781 408 12663 9 (single-user licence)
ISBN 9781 408 12660 8 (site licence)

Printed in Great Britain by Caligraving Ltd, Thetford, Norfolk

Copyright teaching text and compilation © 2011 Gillyanne Kayes, Jeremy Fisher,
Ana Sanderson, Helen MacGregor and Maureen Hanke

Illustrations © 2011 Christiane Engel
Sound recording and film © 2011 A&C Black
Cover illustration by James Watson

Edited by Stephanie Matthews, Laura White and Helen Downer
Designed by Saffron Stocker and Jocelyn Lucas
Sound engineering by Stephen Chadwick
Film and film stills by Walk Tall Media

All rights reserved. No part of this publication may be reproduced or used in
any form or by any means – photographic, electronic or mechanical, including
photocopying, recording, taping or information storage and retrieval systems –
without the prior permission in writing of the publishers.

Single User Licence
The copyright holders have licensed the material in this edition for single use
only. The purchaser/licencee is permitted to use the DVD-ROM at any time on
one terminal only.

Site Licence
The copyright holders have licensed the material in this edition for site use.
The purchaser/ licencee is permitted to use the DVD-ROM simultaneously on
all terminals of the purchasing educational site.

Under the terms of both licences, the purchaser is permitted to make one
exact and unmodified copy of the DVD-ROM in machine-readable form solely
for back up or archival purposes providing this copy is kept in the purchaser's
possession.

Full licence details are included on the DVD-ROM. For any further information
please contact music@acblack.com

Introduction & Help area

Gillyanne Kayes and Jeremy Fisher

Singing is a learned skill, and **Singing Express** uses genre-inclusive and child-inclusive materials to guide children and teachers towards healthy and achievable vocal development.
   Singing Express is underpinned by:
- how children learn in singing;
- five key vocal learning areas;
- an understanding of child vocal development;
- good material for exploring and developing voices;
- tools for monitoring progress and help for teachers;
- realistic examples of when and where to sing.

This can all lead to a happy singing experience in school and, ultimately, for life.

How we learn singing

Singing involves melody, rhythm, words and self-expression. It also requires a degree of physical control in an instrument that changes size, shape and texture, especially in ages 0-20. **Singing Express 4** materials include warm up routines, chants, activities and many different types of song. The approach of the material is: exploration – awareness – control. **Singing Express 4** includes movie demonstrations that will help you to lead and guide the children in some specific techniques used in pitch, body balance and breath and expression.

The singer first, then the song

In **Singing Express** the focus is on developing the singer, rather than learning songs. Music reading is not required for **Singing Express**, although the series includes familiar music or 'song-learning' elements such as melody, pattern, duration, beat, pulse, dynamic and timbre. These are reflected in the guide notes and the learning outcomes.

   Singing Express is written around five key vocal 'learning areas': body balance, breath, pitch, sound shapers and expression. Each learning area is an umbrella term that contains a number of sub-elements. Therefore, **Singing Express 4** contains guide material and specific instruction with regard to breathing, posture and other vocal learning areas.

The child's voice and how it develops

A child's voice is not the same as an adult's; a child's physical-vocal instrument is smaller:
- the lungs are smaller;
- the voice box (larynx) is smaller and in a higher position inside the neck;
- the 'texture' of the vocal fold layers is different.

This means that:
- the pitch range is smaller than an adult's;
- there is less control over pitch in singing than in speaking;
- there is less control over breath, which makes long phrases harder to sing;
- there is less differentiation between the vowel colours;
- the register changes (vocal gear changes in the range) are in a different place.

How we learn to sing 'in tune'

Pitch-matching is a child-friendly way to talk about singing in tune. Pitch-matching can be learned, and requires physical-vocal skill as well as auditory recognition. It is important that teachers are aware of this so that children are not discouraged from enjoying singing at early stages of pitch-matching development.
   Broad signs of development in pitch-matching are:
- awareness of direction in pitch;
- recognition of melodic patterns;
- ability to identify shape of melodic phrase;
- having a process to 'finding your note';
- gaining awareness of how your voice feels in different parts of your vocal range (high and low).

The above are more important than singing the 'right' note. More specifically, children may go through four different phases of development when learning to pitch-match:

Phase 1: Words rather than melody are the centre of interest; singing is likely to be chant-like with a restricted pitch range; falling melodic patterns occur more often.
Phase 2: Developing awareness and conscious control of pitch; able to follow larger melodic contours of a song; sense of musical 'key' is phrase-based; vocal pitch range for song singing expands.
Phase 3: Increased accuracy of melodic shape and intervals, but may change 'key' whilst control of vocal range is still in development.
Phase 4: No significant melodic or pitch errors when singing relatively simple songs of own culture.
('Four stages of development', adapted from Welch, 1998)

   Individual children (and teachers) may be at any one of the above four stages of learning to sing in tune, and you can expect a single class to include children at all of the different stages. **Singing Express** contains a variety of singing material at achievable pitch ranges for each age group so that all children at all stages can participate in, and enjoy, singing.

How to use the vocal learning areas

1. BODY BALANCE

Efficient posture is not about fixing the body in any one position but about recruiting muscles to balance the body against gravity.

   Singing Express 4 offers a selection of energising routines, guided movements, and focusing routines to help children engage physically and mentally for the task of singing. We also identify a 'ready position' when there is a need to be still for singing so that children can discover body balance for themselves. Remember that movements may be modified to suit the needs of children with less mobility, involving arms and shoulders, head, neck and trunk when seated.
   We recommend that you do the routines with the children and also model the 'ready position' when talking about it.

Monitoring progress during body balance

During body balance and energiser routines notice:

- which children seem to enjoy moving about and appear to be well co-ordinated in their movements; are any of the children inhibited in their movements?
- which children seem to follow physical instructions most easily?
- which children seem to be 'trying too hard' because they want to do it 'right'?

Useful movies: 'Ready position' (MD1); 'Listening around you' (MD2); **'Body circles'** (MD6)

2. BREATH

Breath 'control' in singing is really to do with timing: how we time the in-breath to fit with the music and phrase; how we organise the out-breath to fit with the music and phrase. Breathing patterns for singing tend to be different from those in speech because in singing the note is often elongated. Whenever we take a breath in for singing, the tummy needs to be moved out to allow the breath to drop more deeply into the lungs; whenever we breathe out for singing, the tummy needs to be gently pulled in. This helps to squeeze the air and create vibrations in the voice-box that make the pitch. **Singing Express 4** song material has been created with breath-learning in mind, so that children can learn the skill of breathing in during small and large gaps in the music, as well as practising their breathing out skills for shorter and longer phrases.

Monitoring progress during breath

During any singing task notice:

- is the in-breath noisy? This is a sign of strain. Check children's body balance and remind them of 'breathing into their middle'.
- are the children 'filling up' with air every time they take a breath? This is not necessary and can create tension. Discuss the idea of long and short phrases needing different sizes of breath. Remember that children have smaller lungs than you do and that their muscular co-ordination at age eight and nine is not the same as an adult's.
- if any children seem to have a 'reversed' breathing pattern: lifting their chests and pulling their tummies IN when breathing in and pushing their tummies OUT to breathe out. Remind children to 'breathe into their middles' and ask them to place their hands on their tummies to feel how this happens. You might also take them through the body balance and breath routines on the DVD that are helpful for posture and breathing.

Useful movies: 'Breathing into your middle' (MD3); 'Finding space for the in-breath' (MD4); 'Reversed breathing' (MD5); 'Body circles' (MD6)

3. PITCH

Pitch is made when the vocal folds in the voice-box (larynx) vibrate or 'buzz'.

If you put three fingers on the front of your neck and say 'fff' followed by 'vvv' you will feel your voice-box buzzing. Faster vibrations give us a higher pitch; slower vibrations a lower

pitch. In singing we experience this change as high and low in our vocal pitch range. Control of pitch-matching and pitch-range are important singing skills. These skills are not innate – they require experimentation and practice. It is essential to encourage children at all times while they develop these skills.

Singing Express 4 uses a number of different approaches to help children gain conscious control of pitch-matching:

- chants that involve use of high and low speaking voice (eg 'Red riding hood' p22; 'Rain, rain' p41)
- songs that use a very small range of notes with simple melodic patterns (eg 'Step back, baby' p23; 'Let's go Zudie-o' p50)
- songs with multiple verses that are sung on different start notes (eg 'Apples and bananas' p30)
- songs that require a larger pitch range (eg 'The lemon tree' p25; 'Joshua fit the battle of Jericho' p26; 'Supersonic' p51)
- Songs that introduce rounds and simple part-singing (eg 'Chitter chatter' p40; 'Three two one' p34; 'Step back, baby'/'Chicka hanka' pp23-24)

Additionally we have created four movie demonstrations to help you and the children with finding notes (see the Pitch section on the DVD).

Control of pitch-range

Exploration and eventual control of range are a sub-element of pitch learning. There are important links between the pitch of children's speaking voices and their singing range. Here are expected pitches ranges of children's speaking voices and their comfortable singing range taken from a recent survey of the National Singing Programme (Welch et al., 2009):

- Pitch of children's speaking voice:

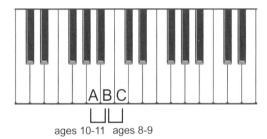

ages 10-11   ages 8-9

When children are learning to sing it is important that they stay mostly within their comfortable singing range so that they can gain confidence and control.

- Comfortable singing range:

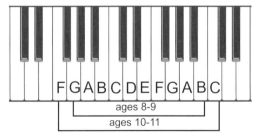

Monitoring progress in pitch

- Chanting: which children enjoy exploring their pitch range in chanting? Talk with them about 'high and low voices' to help their understanding of direction in pitch.

- Anticipating: which children are good at anticipating start notes in echo songs and songs where melodies overlap (eg 'Hocketting' p37; 'Ignition lightspeed' p53); which are having difficulty? You can help them by asking each group to hum and then sing 'in their heads' (ie with no sound) while the other group are singing their lines.
- Control of simple melodic patterns: songs which have a melody of four to six notes are achievable for most children. Using Welch's 'Four stages of pitch-matching' notice which child is at which stage during the school year. Remember that not all children will be at the same stage.
- Control of pitch when the start note changes: which children are able to sense that the tune is the same, even if the start note is higher or lower? Does anyone have difficulty with the highest start note/lowest start note? This will tell you something about children's control of range and pitch.
- Range: sometimes children will 'change key' when a song has a wide pitch range (eg 'The lemon tree' p25; 'Joshua fit the battle of Jericho' p26). They may sing the correct melodic shape but on the 'wrong' notes. Talk with them about the melody going higher/lower and show them how to glide to the correct note in the song.

Useful movies: 'Finding your note – Gliding and landing' (MD7); 'Finding your note –Stepping and jumping' (MD8); 'Finding your note – Singing together' (MD9); Hocketting (MD10)

4. SOUND SHAPERS

The tube of our voice is like any other tube – if we blow or talk through it the sound will 'resonate'. Our mouth, jaw and lips play in important part in shaping the sound, articulating vowels and consonants (essential in language skills) and conveying words in singing. **Singing Express** materials contain poems and chants that explore alliteration and assonance, and tongue twisters that help us to work the muscles that are involved in articulation. So long as the meaning and message of the song gets across it does not matter what accent we use in singing: everyday speaking pronunciation is fine.

Monitoring progress in sound shapers

- Which children are good at exploring sounds that belong together (eg 'The swing (moods of life)' p29]?
- Which children are good at changing consonant or vowel onsets; which are having difficulty? You can help by reminding them of their phonics learning and practising the lines of the song slowly in spoken voice before singing (eg 'Apples and bananas' p30).
- Which children are good at inventing new rhymes? This may tell you something about their language and literacy skills.
- Which children enjoy songs and rhymes with a tongue-twister element (eg 'Gobbledigook' p39)?
- Which children are able to convey songs and chants with complex lyrics clearly? Notice if children are opening their jaw too wide when 'trying' too hard to articulate. You can help them by getting them to mouth the words like a ventriloquist and then making a bigger mouth movement for the important words in the phase.

You can also use songs that indicate sound-shaper learning to monitor children's progress in language skills. Notice:

- if any children are having difficulty in making particular sounds (usually consonants);

- if there are any sounds that individual children are mixing up.

5. EXPRESSION

We sing for a reason: to express ourselves, to tell or remember a story, to create a mood.

Sound effects, tone of voice (timbre) and volume (dynamic) all contribute to expression in singing. These help us to deliver a narrative, create characters, convey emotions and sometimes just have fun with our voice as an instrument. In singing, tone of voice enables us to express the feeling behind the words; there is no one tone of voice that is better than another for singing. Volume enables us to change the impact of a note within a particular phrase, or a phrase within a whole song. Children are less able to control volume in singing than adults.

In **Singing Express 4** there are opportunities for exploration, developing awareness and for control of this important sub-element of expression.

Monitoring progress in expression

- Sound effects and vocal improvisation: which children are good at inventing sound effects and improvising melodic and rhythmic patterns? Which prefer to copy; like to make their sounds individually; are shy or only wanting to explore within the group sound?
- Storytelling: which children get involved in the story of the song; do any children draw back from the singing element of a story song?
- Emotions: which children seem to be expressing emotion through singing; are expressing emotion differently in singing from their normal way (eg 'Goodbye song' p43)?
- Tone of voice: which children are good at exploring and recognise different tones of voice in speaking; which are good at creating different tones of voice in singing (eg 'Tales of long ago and far away' p19; 'The next train to Crewe' p42)? Do any children seem to be 'stuck' with one tone of singing voice – for example, breathy and quiet/loud and strong/sweet and lyrical? Help them by discussing different tones of voice (timbres) heard on the **Singing Express 4** recorded material
- Volume control: which children seem to have only one dynamic (loud/quiet)? Encourage them to make a physical movement to match their sense of how loud the sound is as shown in the movie demo 'Volume control' (MD11).

Where and when, getting started, moving on

In the notes at the start of each theme and under the 'Where and when' headings on the page, you will find helpful suggestions for integrating the activities into other subjects and where in the school you might use them.

Each item offers suggestions for 'Getting started' and for 'Moving on'. These ways in and through the material are for you to take and modify to suit your own individual teaching methods and situations.

Singing Express Songbooks

The **Singing Express** scheme is supported by a separately available, complete set of songbooks for music readers. These contain the songs from the associated **Singing Express** pack in staff notation with piano accompaniments, guitar chords and a CD of song performance tracks.

using the singing express pack

THE DVD-ROM ~ a digital copy of the book

The **Singing Express 4** DVD-ROM contains a digital copy of this book in a format suitable for display on a computer screen or whiteboard. The digital copy is in pdf format and opens in Acrobat Reader (Version 6 or later). (If Acrobat Reader is not installed on your computer, you will need to download and install the appropriate version for your computer in order to open the pdf.)

The DVD-ROM window which opens on launch contains a START pdf, from which you can navigate to any part of the **Singing Express 4** content.

The pdf page for each activity (see sample below) contains embedded audio and movie files and extra whiteboard displays accessed by clicking on the associated icon. When a movie icon is selected, the movie opens (and can be closed) within the document. It has controls for play, pause, fast forward and back, etc. When an audio icon is selected, a small player window opens, giving you controls as above. In addition some of the movies have a drop down menu (to the right of the progress bar) which enables you to select individual verses of songs.

THE DVD-ROM ~ audio and movie files

Also on the DVD-ROM are located all the source files for the embedded movies and audio. You can open these directly – instead of through the activity pdf. Simply click on the file and your computer's default media player will launch the movie or audio. There is a chart of all the audio and movie file names on page 64.

QUICKTIME AV CONTROLS

There are some advantages in selecting Quicktime as the player for opening the audio files directly from the DVD-ROM. Quicktime has a feature called AV (audio visual) Controls, which enables you to raise and lower the pitch, or speed up and slow down the playback. This is particularly useful for starting a song on a higher or lower note, as recommended in many activities. Slowing up the audio may also be useful if any of the children are finding the recorded speed too challenging. Please note that the new version of Quicktime supplied with Mac OS Snow Leopard v. 10.6.1.4 does not include AV controls. If your operating system is using Snow Leopard v. 10.6.1.4 you will need to follow these instructions: http://support.apple.com/kb/ht3678

THE AUDIO CD

The **Singing Express 4** Audio CD contains all the audio performance tracks for those times when you wish to access them with a conventional CD player. The track numbers are listed on page 64.

THE SINGING EXPRESS WEBSITE

The **Singing Express** website – which offers additional support including a HELP area – can be launched from the DVD-ROM by selecting the link located on each page, or by going to www.singingexpress.co.uk

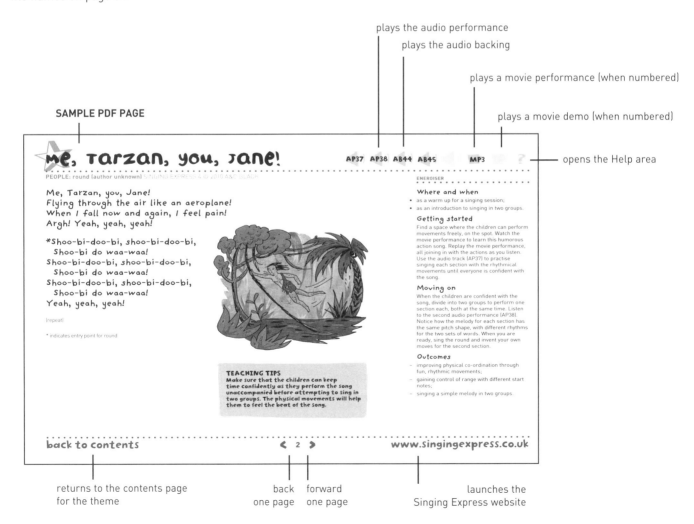

plays the audio performance

plays the audio backing

plays a movie performance (when numbered)

plays a movie demo (when numbered)

SAMPLE PDF PAGE

opens the Help area

returns to the contents page for the theme

back one page

forward one page

launches the Singing Express website

Environment

Body circles

08

LEARNING AREAS: **BODY BALANCE; BREATH**

A sequence of actions, words and sounds that calms the children and focuses their attention on breathing and physical balance. Watch the movie demo to learn the sequence. This is an excellent way to support learning about breathing in science, to prepare the class for the start of an afternoon or to explain about breathing in PE.

Sound map

09

LEARNING AREAS: **SOUND SHAPERS**

Follow an agreed route around the school or any chosen environment and record the sounds you hear. Back in the classroom listen to and discuss the sounds (can the children recognise them?) and copy them vocally. This activity can serve to start a discussion on the difference between sound effects, music and sound effects made into music.

Breathing and breezing along

10

LEARNING AREAS: **BREATH**

This song is all about breathing: why we breathe, how we breathe and what sort of conditions we need for breathing. Children are guided to place their hands on their tummies to feel the movements for the in- and out-breath as they sing.

Under the bridge

11

LEARNING AREAS: **PITCH; EXPRESSION**

Both real bridges and symbolic bridges are a fascinating source of study. This song is about an imagined brick bridge: what lives in its bricks, what travels over it, what flows under it and what passes nearby? Children can be inspired both in design and technology and in an art lesson either by the bridge in the song or by a bridge near to their school.

Tumble down

12

LEARNING AREAS: **PITCH; SOUND SHAPERS**

This reflective song is inspirational in creating an historic mystery surrounding a neglected building. The song is rich with the possibility of exploring rhyme and assonance whilst considering a vital question – what was the building and who lived there?

Water water everywhere

13

LEARNING AREAS: **PITCH; BODY BALANCE**

A song that stresses the importance of water geographically and reminds the singer to take care and not waste water. Children can create actions for accessing water throughout the world (eg water pumps, taps, water carrying) and add them to the song. This is a great song to use in geography and can also be used as the nucleus of a dance/movement composition.

Global warming

14

LEARNING AREAS: **BODY BALANCE; PITCH**

A simple song that teaches about the seasons and their natural activity whilst also bringing attention to the negative affects of global warming. Verses one and three are the same with a contrasting middle verse and there are suggested movements that the children can follow. The song can be a good start for a music composition and makes a strong bridge between learning in geography and the arts.

Endangered species

15

LEARNING AREAS: **SOUND SHAPERS; EXPRESSION**

This big rap about strong animals is a great starting point for learning about ecology systems and animal conservation. It is also a really accessible way for children to be absorbed in rhyme, narration and expression. Challenge the class to write a new verse for the rap.

What's it worth, planet Earth?

16

LEARNING AREAS: **BREATH; PITCH; EXPRESSION**

A catchy song with repeated sections that are easy to learn and effective in performance. In a musical, uplifting and engaging way, this song raises lots of issues about personal responsibility and integrity, linking with the issues facing green schools eg turning lights off, energy prefects, recycling and turning off taps.

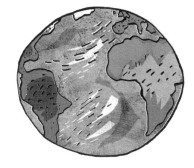

MD1 MD6 ?

ENVIRONMENT: energiser (JF, GK)

Part one:

Cup your hands, turn, and make a small circle.
Cup your hands, turn, and make a bigger
  circle.
Cup your hands, turn, and make the biggest
  circle.

Cup, turn, small circle.
Cup, turn, bigger circle.
Cup, turn, biggest circle.

My circle.
Our circle.
Everybody's circle,
And READY!

Part two:

My circle.
Our circle.
Everybody's circle.

1 2
1 2 3 4
1 2 3 4 5 6

ff,
ffff,
ffffff.

And READY!

LEARNING AREAS: BODY BALANCE; BREATH

Where and when

- as a preparation for singing;
- as part of understanding breathing and physical balance in PE and science;
- as a relaxation exercise to start the afternoon.

Getting started

Watch the first half of the movie demo MD6 ('Cup your hands, turn and make a small circle...'). When the arm movements are familiar, join in with them. The sequence of moves happens three times. Find the 'ready position' at the end (see MD1).

Moving on

Explore the out-breath with the second half of the movie demo MD6. The arm movements are the same. Chant each line in one breath:

1 2 (on one out-breath)

1 2 3 4 (on a longer out-breath)

1 2 3 4 5 6 (on the longest out-breath)

Notice how the 'ff' sound becomes more extended during the sequence of moves.

Outcomes

- making controlled movements while exploring out-breath;
- feeling engaged and ready to sing;
- developing awareness of the extended out-breath.

Sound map

ENVIRONMENT: activity (Kirsty Young)

Where and when

- as an introduction to composition;
- as part of a project on noise pollution;
- as part of philosophy question: can sound effects be music?

Getting started

Supply a group of 'sound explorers' with a sound recording device, notebooks and a map or route to follow. The children follow the route, recording the sounds they hear and noting where they hear them on the map. Several sounds might be heard at once in some locations.

Moving on

Back in the classroom, the sound explorers listen to their recorded sounds and remember where they heard them. Can they use their voices to imitate the sounds? Some sounds might need more than one child to make them. Where several sounds were heard at once, they need to decide who will make which sounds.

The children choose a leader. The leader points to the map and slowly leads the others on a journey. Can the others make the sounds they heard on the journey as the leader points?

Ask other children in the class to listen. Can they work out (without the map) where the leader is taking them on the journey?

Outcomes

- listening to sounds in our environment;
- developing the skill of vocal imitation.

ENVIRONMENT: song (Barry Gibson)

Breathing, *sh* (breathe in)

Just breathing, *sh* (breathe in)

We breathe in the morning, we breathe in
    the night,

We breathe when it's dark and we breathe
    when it's light,

We breathe without thinking, so breathe on,
    that's right,

Breathing, *sh* (breathe in)

Breathing, *sh* (breathe in)

Breathing and breezing along.

Breathing, *ff* (breathe in)

Just breathing, *ff* (breathe in)

It keeps our hearts beating and bumping along,

It keeps our blood bubbling and pumping
    and strong,

It gives us the oomph to keep singing this song,

Breathing, *ff* (breathe in)

Breathing, *ff* (breathe in)

Breathing and breezing along.

Breathing, *ss* (breathe in)

Just breathing, *ss* (breathe in)

The smells and the smoke over here,
    over there,

And coughing and wheezing ~ it just isn't fair,

So let's do our best to breathe lots of
    clean air,

Breathing, *ss* (breathe in)

Breathing, *ss* (breathe in)

Breathing and breezing along.

LEARNING AREAS: BREATH

Where and when

- in science when learning about our bodies and breathing;
- in a music lesson focusing on good breathing practice in singing.

Getting started

Think about activities in which breathing plays a key part (eg swimming, playing a wind instrument, lighting a fire). Listen to the song. Each verse features a 'fricative' sound: 'sh', 'ff', 'ss', followed by an in-breath taken in time with the beat of the song. Join in with the fricative sounds and take an in-breath after each. Put your hands on your tummy to feel how it moves as you do this.

Moving on

Learn the song, making sure to include the fricative sounds. Then watch the movie demo MD3. Discuss with the children if there are 'big spaces' or 'small spaces' for the in-breath at the end of each phrase. All sing the song again, with hands placed on tummies to feel in-breath (tummy moves out) and out-breath (tummy pulls in).

Outcomes

- learning about breathing for singing in a conscious way;
- timing breath between phrases.

TEACHING TIPS

This is a good opportunity to monitor the children's progress in breathing for singing. Who is lifting their shoulders and upper chest to breathe in (this creates unnecessary tension)? Does anyone have a reversed breathing pattern — pushing their tummy out to sing and pulling their tummy in to breathe in (see MD5)?

under the bridge

ENVIRONMENT: song (Barry Gibson)

Under the bridge, ferns and mosses,
Under the bridge, dappled light,
Under the bridge, fish and water,
Under the old, brick bridge.

Near by the bridge, cars and buses,
Near by the bridge, factory town,
Near by the bridge, lorries rumbling,
Near by the old, brick bridge.

Down at the bridge, shimmering water,
Down at the bridge, peace and quiet,
Down at the bridge, soft reflections,
Down at the old, brick bridge.

Over the bridge, loud vibrating,
Over the bridge, iron and steel,
Over the bridge, train wheels rattling,
Over the old, brick bridge.

Under the bridge, ferns and mosses,
Under the bridge, dappled light,
Under the bridge, fish and water,
Under the old, brick bridge.

LEARNING AREAS: PITCH; EXPRESSION

Where and when

- when learning about bridges in design and technology;
- in art as a stimulus for painting.

Getting started

Look at pictures of as many different bridges as possible and discuss their purpose. Listen to the song and join in with the beginning of each line: 'Under the bridge', 'Near by the bridge', 'Down at the bridge' etc. Notice that the volume and tone of each verse reflects the use and environment of the bridge.

Moving on

Find a bridge near school and create your own version of the song 'Under the bridge'. If you don't have a bridge near your school, use an imaginary bridge or one or more well-known bridges (eg Tower Bridge or Tyne Bridge). Be as creative as you want: for example, each verse of the song may represent a different period in history.

Outcomes

- being expressive with words in a verse structure;
- practising pitch-matching to a seven-note melody;
- using changes in tone of voice and volume to create moods.

TEACHING TIPS
The words in the song paint a series of pictures. Can the children use changes of volume and tone of voice to match the mood of each one?

Tumble down

ENVIRONMENT: song (Barry Gibson)

Oh, tumble, tumble down,
Bricks fall and crumble down,
Roll, rubble, roll on down,
Oh, tumble down.

Oh, tumble, tumble down,
Wood creaking, crumble down,
Beams bending, leaning down,
Oh, tumble down.

Oh, tumble, tumble down,
Old building, crumble down,
Time passing, up and down,
Oh, tumble down.

LEARNING AREAS: PITCH; SOUND SHAPERS

Where and when

- in literacy when exploring rhyme and assonance;
- in drama and literacy (eg What is the building? How old is it? Why is it falling down?);
- when using ICT in a music lesson (see 'Moving on' activity).

Getting started

Listen to the song and join in with the first and last lines. Then learn the second and third line of each verse. Enjoy the rhyming words. Sing the whole song; notice that the start notes of verses 2 and 3 are lower.

Moving on

Collect some sound bites of the sounds used in the song (bricks tumbling, beams leaning, wood creaking etc). Create and record a descriptive sound collage to perform around the song.

Outcomes

- exploring a lyrical tone of voice in singing;
- pitch-matching to a five-note melody;
- exploring range by singing a tune starting on a different note for each verse;
- enjoying the sound and feel of rhyme and assonance in verse.

TEACHING TIPS
Help the children access a lyrical singing voice by asking them to say the final phrase of each verse, 'Oh, tumble down', in a sad or slightly disappointed tone of voice. Singing the phrase in this tone of voice will match with the wistful feel of the song.

water water everywhere

ENVIRONMENT: song (David Moses)

Water water everywhere,
You'd think there'd be enough.
It fills the rivers, lakes and seas,
There's plenty of the stuff.
    But some parts of the planet,
    With a dry and sunny clime,
    Get rain just once or twice a year,
    Not pouring all the time.

Water water everywhere,
You'd think there'd be enough.
It fills the rivers, lakes and seas,
There's plenty of the stuff.
    But when the rains don't happen,
    That's what we call a drought.
    No food, no drink, no kitchen sink,
    They have to go without.

Water water everywhere,
You'd think there'd be enough.
It fills the rivers, lakes and seas,
There's plenty of the stuff.
    Next time you turn the tap on,
    Have a care and think again.
    Fresh water is a precious thing,
    Don't pour it down the drain.

Water water everywhere,
Yet still there's not enough.
But everyone could have some,
If we're careful with the stuff.

LEARNING AREAS: BODY BALANCE; PITCH

Where and when
- in a geography session about climates;
- as a stimulus in dance.

Getting started
Listen to the song and join in the 'Water water everywhere' section. Make some gentle wave shapes each time you sing the section.

Moving on
Sing the song, adding actions in the four lines of the repeated 'Water water everywhere' section. Think of three water actions (eg pumping water, carrying it in buckets on heads and drinking). Divide the whole class into three groups and allocate an action to each group. Each time the water section comes around perform the actions simultaneously and change actions for each verse. On the final verse all the children mime a water pump action with two hands.

Outcomes
- gaining confidence in pitch-matching to a six-note melody;
- improving recognition of melodic shape and pattern through repeated notes, patterns and sequences;
- enjoying making movements that match melodic shapes.

TEACHING TIPS
This song has repeated melodic patterns and sequences that are linked to the message of the lyrics: whenever the lyrics talk about water, the melodic shape curves up and down; whenever the lyrics talk about lack of water, the melodic pattern is more static. Can the children be expressive with the words that match with these different melodic patterns?

Global warming

ENVIRONMENT: song (David Sheppard)

APS)) ABS)) ?

Winter, spring and summer and autumn,
Wait for leaves to cover the ground.
Snow and sun take turns to remind us,
Nature's seasons circle around.

Every year the winter gets warmer,
Ozone layers drifting apart.
Ice caps melting, sea levels rising,
Waiting for new patterns to start.

Winter, spring and summer and autumn,
Wait for leaves to cover the ground.
Snow and sun take turns to remind us,
Nature's seasons circle around.

LEARNING AREAS: BODY BALANCE; PITCH

Where and when

- in a geography session about seasons;
- in a music session as a composition.

Getting started

This song has three sections. Listen to the song and ask the children what is different about the second section? (The second section has different words to the other sections; it has the same melody but is one note higher.) Listen to the song and learn the first section (which is repeated as the third section).

Moving on

Add movement to the song: create two circles of children, one inside the other, each circle facing away from the other. The two circles start moving sideways, one step at a time, in time with the beat and in opposite directions. The outer circle stops to sing the first and third sections, whilst the inner circle keeps moving. The inner circle stops to sing the second section, whilst the outer circle keeps moving.

Outcomes

- improving pitch-making skills in a seven-note melody;
- gaining recognition of melodic pattern in a sequence that repeats;
- adding group movements and steps to a song.

TEACHING TIPS
Use this song to observe children's progress in pitch-making (see p3). Which children recognise that the same pattern is repeated three times? Who needs help with this?

Endangered Species

ENVIRONMENT: rap (Matthew Holmes)

Silverback mountain gorilla,
On the forest slopes, foraging for dinner,
Eats his way through piles of vegetation,
But along come the loggers,
TIMBER! Devastation.
Tall trees fall where the silverback roams,
Where are these gorillas gonna make
   their homes?

  Silverback, silverback,
  Then there were none.
  There'll be no gorillas,
  When the last one's gone.
  Gone...gone...gone...

Grizzly bear, fearsome creature,
With his claws and teeth, brown,
  furry features,
Eight feet tall, enormous appetite,
But along comes the hunter,
BANG! He's in his sight.
Frightened beast through the wilderness runs,
Still there's no escaping from the
  hunters' guns.

  Grizzly bear, grizzly bear...
  There'll be no more grizzlies...

Leatherback turtles swim
Across the ocean waves, two metre flippers.
Diving for a jellyfish for tea,
But the trawler net will
HAUL HIM from the sea.
Fishermen, must the leatherback fear?
Do we have to wait until they disappear?

  Leatherback, leatherback...
  There'll be no more turtles...

LEARNING AREAS: SOUND SHAPERS; EXPRESSION

Where and when

- learning about world conservation;
- learning about ecology systems.

Getting started

Listen to the rap (AD1). Feel the beat and the rhythm of the words. Listen out for these words: 'TIMBER!' in Verse 1, 'BANG!' in Verse 2 and 'HAUL HIM' in Verse 3. Discuss how they stand out. Join in with these words and find a movement that will go with the word (eg 'TIMBER!': arms up high and gradually bend from the waist with a flop down to finish, 'BANG!': two hands raised very quickly in defence of a bullet). Join in with the chorus each time it comes.

Moving on

Learn the whole rap. Enjoy chanting the words with the beat. Notice which words come on a strong beat. Also notice words that are stretched out or spoken quickly.

Invent a new verse using another endangered species, eg Bengali tiger.

Outcomes

- enjoying the rhythms, sounds and stress of words as part of a rap;
- exploring rap as a form of narrative expression.

what's it worth, planet Earth?

ENVIRONMENT: song (Suzy Davies)

All chant: **Reduce, re-use, recycle.** (x4)

All sing:

What's it worth, planet Earth?
Tell me, what does it mean to you?
What's it worth, planet Earth?
Tell me, what are you prepared to do?

It only takes a second to turn off the tap,
While you're brushing your pearly whites.
It only takes a tick and a flick of the wrist,
To switch off unnecessary lights.
This beautiful, blue green paradise,
Should be the pride of the universe.
So, whoever you are, whatever you do,
Let's put the planet first.

What's it worth, planet Earth...

If you're not going far, why get in the car?
Ride the bus and enjoy the view.
Or why not take a hike? Maybe get on
    your bike?
You'll do your health a favour too.
This beautiful blue green paradise,
Should be the pride of the universe.
So, whoever you are, whatever you do,
Let's put the planet first.

Chant:

Group 1: **Reduce**

Group 2: **Look for less packaging on the products that you use.**

Group 1: **Re-use**

Group 2: **Don't just chuck away something someone else could use.**

Group 1: **Recycle**

Group 2: **Could your rubbish be reborn as something new?**

All: **Reduce, re-use, recycle.**

All sing: **What's it worth, planet Earth...** (x2)

LEARNING AREAS: BREATH; PITCH; EXPRESSION

Where and when

- in a geography session about climate;
- in an RE lesson about personal integrity and responsibility.

Getting started

Listen to the song. The phrase 'Reduce, re-use, recycle' is repeated four times at the beginning, getting slightly louder each time. Watch the movie demo then join in with the audio performance making the arm movements to show the changes in volume.

Moving on

Learn the whole song. Where indicated in the lyrics, divide the children into two groups. Group 1 chants Part 1 ('Reduce, re-use, recycle') and Group 2 chants Part 2 ('Look for less packaging...'). The children could also invent their own phrases for this section for Group 2 to perform.

Outcomes

- gaining confidence in pitch-matching skills through moving from chant to pitch;
- controlling pitch in a seven-note melody;
- learning to time the in-breath with the rhythm of the music;
- learning to control volume as a means of expression in song.

TEACHING TIPS
Set the volume level of the song chorus to relatively low using the movie demo as a guide. This will help the children access the highest notes ('to do') without vocal strain.

Narrative

Throw it out the window 18

ENERGISER

As they sing this nonsense song the children have fun playing with the words of well-known nursery rhymes. It provides a good starting point for sharing the nursery rhymes they know and then making up more silly verses of their own to sing together.

Tales of long ago and far away 19

LEARNING AREAS: **BREATH; PITCH; EXPRESSION**

A charming, lyrical song which uses phrases that are commonly found in traditional tales, eg 'Once upon a time...' The song is ideal for singing as the opener or ending of any musical performance of a traditional tale.

Jack and the beanstalk 20

LEARNING AREAS: **BREATH; EXPRESSION**

This energetic rap recounts the main events in the traditional tale and gives lots of opportunity for using expressive voices. The children will enjoy finding a suitable voice for the giant's infamous 'Fee fi fo fum' chant! A lively re-telling that would be perfect for performance in assembly or a school show.

Red Riding Hood 22

LEARNING AREAS: **PITCH; EXPRESSION**

Another fun rap version of a traditional tale. Its use of adjectives at the end of each verse makes it a good chant for integrating into literacy teaching. There is lots of opportunity for expressive use of voice in performance to create a dramatic re-telling.

Step back, baby ~ Chicka hanka

23–24

LEARNING AREAS: **BODY BALANCE; PITCH**

Two traditional action songs that can be performed by two groups at the same time as 'partner' songs to introduce part-singing skills. 'Step back, baby' tells a funny story, while the regular rhythm of 'Chicka Hanka' matches the train described in the song. Both songs are often sung as playground songs.

The lemon tree 25

LEARNING AREAS: **PITCH; EXPRESSION**

A beautiful Bengali wedding song describing the wedding presents the groom offers to his bride. This is an excellent song for incorporating with learning about wedding traditions in citizenship, or Hinduism and Indian culture.

Joshua fit the battle of Jericho 26

LEARNING AREAS: **PITCH; EXPRESSION**

A gospel song with a strong beat and simple, descriptive words which tell the Bible story of the battle of Jericho. This arrangement provides lots of opportunity for a vivid performance using vocal sound effects.

Throw it out the window

NARRATIVE: nonsense song (traditional)

Mary had a little lamb,
Its fleece was white as snow,
And everywhere that Mary went,
She threw it out the window,
    The window, the window,
    The second storey window,
    And everywhere that Mary went,
    She threw it out the window.

Old Mother Hubbard
Went to the cupboard,
To fetch her poor dog a bone,
But when she got there, the cupboard was bare,
So she threw it out the window,
    The window, the window,
    The second storey window,
    But when she got there, the cupboard was bare,
    So she threw it out the window.

The grand old Duke of York,
He had ten thousand men,
He marched them up to the top of the hill,
And he threw them out the window,
    The window, the window,
    The second storey window,
    He marched them up to the top of the hill,
    And he threw them out the window.

Yankee Doodle came to town,
Riding on a pony,
He stuck a feather in his cap,
And he threw it out the window,
    The window, the window,
    The second storey window,
    He stuck a feather in his cap,
    And he threw it out the window.

ENERGISER

Where and when
- on a coach journey/school trip;
- in a whole school singing assembly.

Getting started
Ask the children to think of all the nursery rhyme characters they are familiar with and collect the names, reminding the children of the rhyme if necessary. Play the audio track and ask the children to identify the four characters referred to in the verses. Play the track again, all joining in with the chorus ('The window, the window').

Moving on
Together, say the first verse of each traditional nursery rhyme mentioned in the song. Ask the children what has happened to the verses in the song? (The last line has changed to '... threw it out the window'.)

Teach the melody and words of the three verses by singing the lines yourself or using the audio track, then sing the whole song together.

Use other familiar characters and the nursery rhymes the children suggested to create new verses for the song, eg 'Little Jack Horner sat in the corner eating his Christmas pie, He stuck in a thumb and pulled out a plum, And he threw it out the window.'

Outcomes
- having fun with language to give a new 'twist' to old ideas;
- warming up the voice with a game-song.

(handwritten notes) p23 Track 9. Step Back Baby. Track 11 together

Tales of long ago and far away

NARRATIVE: song (Ian Lawrence)

Everybody loves to be told a story,
Children round the world are all the same.
'Once upon a time' we start,
Everybody knows that part,
Tales of long ago and far away.

Everyone believes in a happy ending,
Heroines and heroes save the day.
Everybody loves the end,
Where the villains lose again,
Tales of long ago and far away.

LEARNING AREAS: BREATH; PITCH; EXPRESSION

Where and when
- as an introduction to a class performance of a traditional tale;
- as part of a creative writing lesson.

Getting started
Ask the children to say which words and phrases they think are commonly used at the beginning and end of traditional stories. Listen to 'Tales of long ago and far away' together. How many traditional stories can the children think of which begin with 'Once upon a time...'?

Discuss the title of the song and how it links to the historical settings of many of these stories. Listen again and all join in with the last line of each verse.

Moving on
Learn the song. Then watch the movie demo which shows how the singer finds space for the in-breath between the phrases (MD4). Encourage the children to sing the words smoothly, singing one phrase in one breath where they can.

Outcomes
- practising pitch-matching to a seven-note melody;
- practising finding space for the in-breath;
- finding a lyrical tone of voice.

TEACHING TIPS
This charming song is easier to sing in a lyrical tone of voice. Ask the children to imagine they are singing it to a younger brother or sister — not too loud and with a gentle, soothing quality.

Jack and the beanstalk

NARRATIVE: rap (HM)

Once upon a time, Jack lived with his mother.
He had no dad, no sister, no brother
He did have a cow by the name of Daisy
He sold her for a bean (well, she was
   quite lazy!)

A weird thing happened in the middle of
   the night
A beanstalk grew to an incredible height!
Jack waved goodbye, then climbed up high
He went on up till he reached the sky.

At the top of the beanstalk, he looked around
Saw enormous footprints on the ground
That's when he heard the horrible hum
The giant's voice singing 'Fee fi fo fum.'

   'Fee fi fo fum, fee fi fo fum,
   I smell the blood of an Englishman!'

Jack grabbed some gold when he heard
   that shout,
Ran for the beanstalk 'I better get out!
I won't last long in this giant's town,'
He held on tight and clambered down.

The money didn't last and was soon all spent
'Go get some more to pay the rent,'
Said Mum to Jack (who wasn't very willing
But he had no choice 'cause they didn't have
   a shilling).

At the top of the beanstalk Jack
   looked around,
Saw enormous footprints on the ground.
That's when he heard the horrible hum
The giant's voice singing 'Fee fi fo fum.'

   'Fee fi fo fum, fee fi fo fum,
   I smell the blood of an Englishman!'

(continued)

LEARNING AREAS: BREATH; EXPRESSION

Where and when

- in literacy work when comparing different versions of traditional tales;
- as a performance in an assembly or a concert.

Getting started

Ask the children to recount the main events in the traditional story of 'Jack and the beanstalk'. Teach them the words and rhythms of the giant's chant, 'Fee fi fo fum...', using the audio performance track for reference. Listen to this re-telling of the story and to join in with the giant's chant.

Moving on

Divide the class into ten small groups and give each group four lines of the rap to learn by heart (not including the giant's chant). Ask the groups to find ways of using their voices and faces expressively for their particular section of the story. They may like to add actions or movement to enhance the story.

Perform the rap all the way through, each group taking their turn and everyone joining in for the giant's chant. The children might also like the challenge of learning the whole rap for a class performance.

Outcomes

- co-ordinating words, rhythm and breath;
- using tone of voice and volume for expression.

TEACHING TIPS
Different tones of voice (timbres) in singing are an important element of using our voice expressively. Encourage the children to find distinctive voices for Jack, the Giant, Mother and the narrator.

Jack grabbed Henny, who laid all the money
It started getting scary ~ it wasn't
  very funny
The giant chased Jack right out of town,
He was shaking with fear as he clambered
  down.

Jack was fast when he reached the ground
He picked up the axe as he heard the sound
Of breaking branches and that horrible hum
The giant's voice singing 'Fee fi fo fum.'

  'Fee fi fo fum, fee fi fo fum,
  I smell the blood of an Englishman!'

Jack swung the axe with its shiny blade
Swish chop chop was the sound it made
The beanstalk crashed and the giant fell
The story ends and all was well.

But now and then in the middle of the night
Jack has a dream and wakes with fright
He hears in the distance the horrible hum
The giant's voice singing 'Fee fi fo fum.'

  'Fee fi fo fum, fee fi fo fum,
  I smell the blood of an Englishman!'

Red Riding Hood

NARRATIVE: rap (Helen MacGregor)

Now once upon a time, in a cottage in a wood,
Lived a cute little girl, Red Riding Hood.
CUTE GIRL!

Now one fine day, her mum said to her,
'Just take those goodies to your Grandmother.'
KIND GIRL!

So off she set, through the deep dark wood,
The brave little girl, Red Riding Hood.
BRAVE GIRL!

'Isn't that heavy?' The ugly wolf asked her,
'I'll take them, 'cause I'll get there faster!'
CRAFTY WOLF!

He knocked Granny's door, she shot out of bed,
'Get in the cupboard!' The bad wolf said.
WICKED WOLF!

Along came Little Red Riding Hood,
To see her Grandmother if she could,
'What big ears, big teeth, big eyes!'
Altogether a scary surprise.
UGLY WOLF!

The woodcutter heard Red Riding Hood shout,
So he gave the wolf a jolly big clout.
BRAVE WOODCUTTER!

The wolf was shocked and he took fright,
Out popped Grandma, what a sight.
POOR GRANDMA!

No more wolf to scare them away,
Just a nice big party with time to play.
HOORAY!
HOORAY!

LEARNING AREAS: PITCH; EXPRESSION

Where and when

- at storytime;
- as part of phonics teaching on rhythm and rhyme.

Getting started

Ask the children to re-tell the story of Red Riding Hood, using puppets if you wish.

All listen to the rap on the audio track (AD3). Ask the children what they remember from this version, replaying it if needed. What adjectives are used to describe each character? Invite the children to join in with the last line of each verse, using their voices expressively to match the meaning of each adjective, eg a sweet, light voice for 'CUTE GIRL!' and a scared voice for 'UGLY WOLF!' etc.

Moving on

Give the children opportunities to practise saying some of the characters' speech lines, eg the wolf: 'Get in the cupboard!' Explore different ways of using pitch, volume and the tone of voice to characterise the wolf. Teach the rap, using the whiteboard display of the lyrics if you wish. Encourage the children to develop their own performance or join in with the audio track, using puppets to act out the story if you prefer.

Outcomes

- exploring inflections in pitch for characterisation;
- using different tones of voice to create a dramatic narrative.

TEACHING TIPS
Changing pitch in the spoken voice helps us to develop control and confidence for pitch-matching in singing. Ask the children to make shapes in the air with their hands when a phrase changes pitch, eg 'Lived a cute little girl, Red Riding Hood'. Can they identify when the pitch is moving (up or down)?

Step back, baby

NARRATIVE: song (traditional)

Not last night but the night before.
Step back, baby, step back!
Twenty-four robbers at my door,
Step back, baby, step back!

Open up the door and let them in,
Step back, baby, step back!
Hit 'em on the head with the rollin' pin,
Step back, baby, step back!

Should've seen the way those robbers ran...
Step back, baby, step back!
I picked up my frying pan...
Step back, baby, step back!

Some flew east and some flew west...
Step back, baby, step back!
Some flew over the cuckoo's nest...
Step back, baby, step back!

LEARNING AREAS: PITCH; BODY BALANCE

Where and when

- as a starter for a drama lesson;
- in the playground.

Getting started

Ask the children to listen to the story in 'Step back, baby' as you play the audio track. Can they re-tell the sequence of events told in the lyrics? Who do they think is telling the story? Notice that it is told in the first person.

Join in with the line 'Step back, baby' and the words as they become familiar. Notice that the melody is just three notes and that the first note of each line is the highest of the three.

Moving on

Ask the children to suggest some simple rhythmical actions to match the lyrics, eg mime knocking at the door seven times, hold a 'rolling pin' in the air and mime hitting with it four times on the beat and three footsteps on the spot before the two hand-claps on the refrain.

Encourage the children to sing with energy and determination, like the storyteller who scares off the robbers!

Perform the song unaccompanied as well as with the audio track, aiming to keep a strong regular beat throughout.

Outcomes

- pitch-matching to a three-note melody;
- creating movements to go with a lively song narrative.

TEACHING TIPS
Fitting words with a melody is an important singing skill. Do the children notice that the melodic pattern is the same for each verse but that there are different numbers of syllables to fit in, eg 'Not last night but the'; 'Twenty-four robbers'; 'Open up the door and'? This changes the rhythmic pattern.

Chicka hanka

NARRATIVE: song (traditional)

Captain, go sidetrack your train,
Captain, go sidetrack your train,
Number one on line,
Comin' in on time,
Captain, go sidetrack your train.

(repeat once)

LEARNING AREAS: PITCH; BODY BALANCE

Where and when

- as a physical and vocal warm up for a singing session;
- in a music lesson focusing on two-part singing.

Getting started

This American singing game has a simple repetitive melody with a strong off-beat rhythm which the children sing as they move their arms round to the beat like the wheels of the train. All stand and listen to the song (AP10) as you demonstrate the movement, encouraging the children to copy you and keep to the beat. Join in with the singing as the children become familiar with the simple words and melody.

Moving on

When the children are confident singing both 'Step back, baby' and 'Chicka hanka', they can be sung as partner songs. Listen to the audio performance (AP11) and divide the children into two groups. The children can sing along with the audio performance. Alternatively, sing unaccompanied: start the 'Chicka hanka' group first. When they repeat the song for the second time, then bring in the 'Step back, baby' group.

Outcomes

- gaining confidence in pitch-matching to a four-note melody;
- improving recognition of melodic pattern through repeated and changing melodic patterns;
- learning how two melodies can fit together to make harmony (when partnered with 'Step back, baby').

TEACHING TIPS
The children may need practice and help with finding their note when singing this song as a partner song to 'Step back, baby'. Use the movie demo as a resource to help children gain confidence and skill in this aspect of pitch-matching.

The lemon tree

NARRATIVE: wedding song (traditional Bengali)

Under the lemon tree the happy bridegroom
    dresses himself,
Don't pick the lemons, my dear.
Under the lemon tree the happy bridegroom
    dresses himself,
Don't pick the lemons, my dear.

I will go into the stable,
And pick out the best of all.
Pick out a horse whose teeth are healthy,
For my wife,
Don't pick the lemons, my dear.

    Under the lemon tree...

I will go into the elephant house,
And pick out the best of all.
Pick out an elephant that's strong and mighty,
For my wife,
Don't pick the lemons, my dear.

    Under the lemon tree...

I will go into the hen house,
And pick out the best of all.
Pick out a hen whose eggs are tasty,
For my wife,
Don't pick the lemons, my dear.

LEARNING AREAS: PITCH; EXPRESSION

Where and when

- in geography work about India and the Hindu religion;
- in citizenship discussions about cultural wedding traditions.

Getting started

This is a beautiful Bengali wedding song with a verse and chorus structure. Listen to the song together and ask the children which three presents the bridegroom chooses (a horse, an elephant and a hen). Why do you think the bridegroom warns his wife not to pick the lemons? Perhaps because they are so sour!

Play the song again and all join in with the line 'Don't pick the lemons, my dear'.

Moving on

Teach the whole chorus and then each verse one by one. Aim to sing the whole of the first line in one breath, and use your voices expressively to sing 'Don't pick the lemons, my dear'. When the children are confident with the song, you might like to ask a soloist or a small group of boys to sing this line.

Outcomes

- pitch-matching to a seven-note melody;
- learning to manage melodic patterns that have similar shapes but appear in different parts of the vocal range;
- experiencing how musical structure can be used to express the meaning and feel of a song story.

TEACHING TIPS
The pitch-range of this song enables children to explore their higher voices in the verse section. Who is singing the verse accurately; who is singing the correct shape but on different notes; who is struggling to find their high voice? Help the children glide to the correct notes using the technique of 'gliding and landing' (see MD7).

Joshua fit the battle of Jericho

NARRATIVE: spiritual (traditional)

Joshua fit the battle of Jericho,
Jericho, Jericho,
Joshua fit the battle of Jericho,
And the walls come tumblin' down.

You may talk about your King of Gideon,
You may talk about your man of Saul.
There's none like good ol' Joshua,
At the battle of Jericho.

Joshua fit the battle of Jericho...

Up to the walls of Jericho,
He marched with spear in hand,
'Go blow them ram horns!' Joshua cried,
''Cause the battle is in my hand.'

Group 1 chant:

Left, left,
Left, right, left,
Left, left,
Left, right, left.

(x2)

Group 2 chant (2nd time only):

Baa! Baa!
Baa!
Baa! Baa!
Baa!

All: Joshua fit the battle of Jericho...

Then the ram sheep horns began to blow,
Trumpets began to sound.
Joshua commanded the children to shout,
And the walls come tumblin' down.

Group 1 sing:

Wah dah dah,
Wah dah dah,
Wah dah dah,
Wah dah dah.

(x2)

Group 2 chant (2nd time only):

Jericho!
Jericho!
Jericho!
Jericho!

All: Joshua fit the battle of Jericho...

The walls come tumblin' down. Bang!

LEARNING AREAS: PITCH, EXPRESSION

Where and when

- in RE when exploring Bible stories;
- in a music lesson, when introducing gospel songs.

Getting started

Tell the children the story of Joshua and the battle referred to in the song. Listen to the song and encourage the children to feel the beat by tapping knees and clicking fingers alternately, or marching silently on the spot. Learn the chorus and join in each time it is repeated, noticing how the pitch of the melody moves up and then down in the last phrase. What happens at the very end of the song? (The last line is repeated but is sung moving upwards in pitch.)

Moving on

Learn the verses and divide into two groups to add the layered sound effect sections: 'Left, left, Left, right, left' and 'Baa! Baa! Baa!' after Verse 2 and 'Wah dah dah' and 'Jericho!' after Verse 3. Ask the children how they can use their voices expressively to narrate the story during the song and these sections. They may like to add actions to the sound effects.

Outcomes

- pitch-matching to an eight-note melody;
- learning control of pitch in upward and downward directions;
- exploring a more extended range;
- enjoying song as narrative.

TEACHING TIPS

This song gives the children an opportunity to explore more of their vocal range in the declamatory section 'you may talk'. An excellent way to help the children find the notes for this part of the song is to get them to call out in a high-pitched voice: 'hello'/'hi'/'you may talk'. They can then get the feel of the higher pitch without having to sing it.

Pattern

Rubber chicken 28
ENERGISER
A great way to focus a group that is full of energy, particularly before a PE lesson or at the change of a lesson. Use the movie performance to guide you and enjoy shaking out the fidgets as the count gets progressively shorter.

The swing (moods of life) 29
LEARNING AREAS: **SOUND SHAPERS; EXPRESSION**
A reflective poem by Mary D. Chauhan in which the swing symbolises our changing moods in life. The activities are ideal for both PSHE and for exploring the rich expressive sounds of its words. Create a vocal accompaniment to the poem and imagine it to be the soundtrack for a film then discuss what the film might be about.

Apples and bananas 30
LEARNING AREAS: **PITCH; SOUND SHAPERS**
A song to get your mouth around as each verse focuses on a different vowel sound but always the same words – apples and bananas. The song is great as part of a literacy session and provides a lovely way of playing with words.

All year round 31
LEARNING AREAS: **BREATH; PITCH**
This is a simple but effective song that helps the children grasp wider concepts of the cycles in life such as growth and change, the seasons and the earth's rotation. It is a fine contribution to the geography curriculum.

Fit together 32
LEARNING AREAS: **PITCH; SOUND SHAPERS**
A song to prompt investigation into patterns created by nature and by humans. Some of the words are chanted and the chorus has a simple melody and words with finger-clicking. By discussing the sorts of patterns referred to in the song, children are encouraged to consider patterns in their lives and learning, such as number patterns and relationships in maths.

Nanuma 33
LEARNING AREAS: **PITCH; SOUND SHAPERS**
This traditional Ghanaian song is appropriate for many levels of musical ability. Embracing the strong steady beat it can be sung in unison or as a round in two or four parts. The children can sing on the spot or with strong movements added and the class can enjoy researching about Ghanaian culture.

Three two one 34
LEARNING AREAS: **PITCH**
This jazzy round enables the children to learn to sing in harmony. The words guide the children to the shape of the melody and the melodies fit together as musical patterns and create an attractive harmony.

Beat box rock 35
LEARNING AREAS: **SOUND SHAPERS; EXPRESSION**
A funky song that develops a whole musical language of beat boxing. Children are able to gain confidence in using their voices to imitate the sound of instruments in a band, namely drum kit, bass and lead guitar. Many will be able to beat box their own sounds and teach them to the class. The song makes a great contribution to any performance!

Rubber chicken

PATTERN: energiser (author unknown)

(shake right arm)	One, two, three, four, five, six, seven, eight
(shake left arm)	One, two, three, four, five, six, seven, eight
(shake right leg)	One, two, three, four, five, six, seven, eight
(shake left leg)	One, two, three, four, five, six, seven, eight
(shake right arm)	One, two, three, four
(shake left arm)	One, two, three, four
(shake right leg)	One, two, three, four
(shake left leg)	One, two, three, four
(shake right arm)	One, two
(shake left arm)	One, two
(shake right leg)	One, two
(shake left leg)	One, two
(shake right arm)	One
(shake left arm)	One
(shake right leg)	One
(shake left leg)	One
(shout while waving hands in air)	RUBBER CHICKEN!

ENERGISER

Where and when

- to focus a group into changing activity;
- as part of a PE warm up.

Getting started

Watch the movie performance. When the sequence of moves is familiar, join in. At the end everyone can enjoy yelling out 'Rubber chicken!'

Moving on

Add this to the sequence: each time you start the cycle of movements turn to face ninety degrees left, ending up facing the front.

Outcomes

- finding energy and balance through guided movements.

TEACHING TIPS
Encourage the children to stand in the 'ready position' (see movie demo) before the chant begins: this will help them to maintain balance and enjoy the moves in the activity while speaking at the same time.

The Swing (moods of life)

PATTERN: poem (Mary D. Chauhan)

Oopar niche...tu ichko kai
Tu ichko kai

Oopar niche...oo ichko kam
Oo ichko kam

Oopar niche...tu ichko kai
Oopar niche...oo ichko kam

Tu ichko kai
Oo ichko kam
Oo ichko kam
Tu ichko kai

Oopar niche...
Niche oopar

Oo ichko kam
Oo ichko kam
Tu ichko kai
Tu ichko kai

Oopar niche...niche oopar
Oopar niche...niche oopar

Oo ichko kam
Tu ichko kai
Tu ichko kai
Tu ichko kai
Tu ichko kai
Tu ichko kai
Oo ichko kam.

LEARNING AREAS: SOUND SHAPERS; EXPRESSION

Where and when

- in PSHE to discuss moods;
- as part of a music composition session.

Getting started

Read the poem out loud. Can the children identify anything about it? (It is not in English, it has few phrases, phrases are repeated and it has a slow, steady beat.) Show the children the text and point out the three repeated phrases. The language is Gujarati; it has been written phonetically and means 'Up down...you are swinging'. The lines are not repeated in any particular pattern and sometimes the author writes phrases backwards. Each phrase creates a steady beat to give the feel of a swing. Let the children join in on the words 'Oopar niche' each time it comes and imagine that they are giving someone on a swing a push to get them higher. End the poem by getting quieter until the voice comes to a halt.

Moving on

Using its steady rhythm and its two main sounds 'ooo' and 'eee', create a vocal accompaniment. Make the sounds into a two-note melody that everyone likes; the melody should feel like it is gently swinging up and down. Add the accompaniment when you think it fits, either whilst the poem is being read or in between sections. Imagine the finished composition as the opening music to a film; what would the film be about?

Outcomes

- enjoying the shapes and sounds of a different language (Gujarati);
- exploring patterns of words and sounds;
- improvising a melodic pattern.

Apples and bananas

PATTERN: nonsense song (traditional)

I like to eat, eat, eat, eat,
I like to eat, apples and bananas,
I like to eat, eat, eat, eat,
I like to eat, apples and bananas.

I like to ayt, ayt, ayt, ayt,
I like to ayt, aypples and baynaynays,
I like to ayt, ayt, ayt, ayt,
I like to ayt, aypples and baynaynays.

I like to eet, eet, eet, eet,
I like to eet, eeples and beeneenees,
I like to eet, eet, eet, eet,
I like to eet, eeples and beeneenees.

I like to ite, ite, ite, ite,
I like to ite, iples and bininis,
I like to ite, ite, ite, ite,
I like to ite, iples and bininis.

I like to ote, ote, ote, ote,
I like to ote, oples and bononos,
I like to ote, ote, ote, ote,
I like to ote, oples and bononos.

I like to oot, oot, oot, oot,
I like to oot, ooples and boonoonoos,
I like to oot, oot, oot, oot,
I like to oot ooples and boonoonoos.

Now we're through, through, through, through,
Now we're through with the apples and bananas,
Now we're through, through, through, through,
With A, E, I, O, U.

LEARNING AREAS: SOUND SHAPERS; PITCH

Where and when

- in literacy to practise vowel sounds;
- packing away before break or lunch.

Getting started

Check out the vowel sounds A, E, I, O, U with the class. Listen to the song and discuss why it is funny (each verse uses a different vowel sound). Join in the song, carefully singing the changed sounds.

Moving on

Develop the nonsense part of the song by substituting other foods that work well, eg coconuts and mangos. Children could play with sounds even more by then swapping the starting sound, eg 'Coconuts and mangos' becomes 'Moconuts and cangos'. Some may develop a whole new language.

Outcomes

- gaining confidence in pitch-matching by singing a simple six-note melody on different start notes;
- practising articulation by using a different vowels with the same syllable.

TEACHING TIPS
Use this fun song to observe children's progress in pitch-matching (see p3). The song uses four different start notes that are progressively higher. You may like to use the movie demo (MD7) to help the children find the progressively higher notes for each verse. Do any of the children have difficulty with the highest or lowest versions? This will tell you something about their skill with range, which is part of pitch-matching.

All year round

PATTERN: song (Barry Gibson)

All year round, all year round,
All year round, all year round,
All year round, all year round,
All year round, all year round.

Seasons turn, all year round,
World spins on, all year round,
Winds they blow, all year round,
Plants they grow, all year round.

Raindrops fall, all year round,
Creatures call, all year round,
Give and take, all year round,
Sleep and wake, all year round.

Warm to cold, young to old,
What to do? Old to new!
You and me, energy,
Cycling round, all year round.

All year round, all year round,
All year round, all year round,
All year round, all year round,
All year round, all year round.

LEARNING AREAS: BREATH; PITCH

Where and when

- in geography when discussing weather and seasons;
- as part of understanding the cycle of celebrations, eg harvest, birthdays, anniversaries etc.

Getting started

Discuss what marks out a year for us (the 12 months, our birthdays, the seasons etc). Listen to the song and learn verse 1. Listen to the rest of the song and join in the 'All year round' phrase. What other examples of things happening annually does the song use? (Seasons, world spins, plants, waking and sleeping etc.)

Moving on

All the phrases in this song are the same length; there is a space at the end of each phrase for an in-breath. Ask the children to place their hands on their tummies (see Help area, p4/MD5) to feel the movement on the in-breath. Do they need a big breath or a small breath to sing these phrases? (Quite small breath as the phrases are short.)

Outcomes

- gaining confidence with melodic patterns that repeat and change;
- practising pitch-matching to a seven-note melody;
- practising finding space and moving the tummy correctly for the in-breath.

TEACHING TIPS
Sometimes when we focus on breathing, our tummy moves the wrong way (see Help area and the movie demo). Notice if any children are doing this and encourage them to let their tummies move out as they breathe in, and keep their shoulders relaxed.

Fit together

PATTERN: song (Barry Gibson)

Sing: (click click) **Fit together,** (click click) **fit together,**
We're looking for the patterns, see them
(click click) **fit together.**

Chant: The tiniest of particles, the atom, or
the quark,
The minusculest molecule, the flicker in
the dark.

Sing: We're looking for the patterns
And they're somehow connected
See them fit together, fit together.

Sing: (click click) **Fit together,** (click click) **fit together,**
Life is for living, see it (click click) **fit together.**

Chant: The wings on a butterfly, a leaf upon
a tree,
The weaving of a spider's web, the hands
on you and me.

Sing: We're looking for the patterns...

Sing: (click click) **Fit together,** (click click) **fit together,**
Worlds are for turning, see them (click click)
fit together.

Chant: The earth, the moon, the sun, the planets,
always changing place,
The spinning stars, the galaxies that spiral
on in space.

Sing: We're looking for the patterns...

Sing: (click click) **Fit together,** (click click) **fit together,**
We're looking for the patterns, see them
(click click) **fit together.**

Chant: The shapes that keep repeating and the
numbers that surprise,
The dots, the lines, the zig-zags dancing
right before our eyes.

Sing: We're looking for the patterns...

Sing: (click click) **Fit together,** (click click) **fit together** (x3)
Chant: **Fit together!**

LEARNING AREAS: PITCH; SOUND SHAPERS

Where and when

- when working on natural sciences and the world around us;
- in maths when learning about number patterns.

Getting started

Talk about patterns you can see in the classroom (eg floor tiles, windows etc) and patterns outside (eg spider's web, tree trunk rings). Listen to the song and see how many patterns the children can remember. Learn the first two lines and the chorus joining in with the finger clicks.

Moving on

Learn the spoken phrases in each verse. Make sure that the children use their sound shapers – lips, teeth and tongue – to articulate the words clearly. They may need to listen to the audio performance a few times to fit the words with the rhythmic pattern.

Outcomes

- practising control of pitch-matching with the smallest step between two notes in an eight-note melody;
- moving from speaking to singing in rhythm.

Nanuma

Pattern: Ghanaian song (traditional)

Nanuma wyaeh, Nanuma,
*Nanuma wyaeh, Nanuma,
*Nanuma wyaeh, Nanuma,
*Nanuma wyaeh, Nanuma.

(repeat once)

* indicates entry point for round

LEARNING AREAS: PITCH; SOUND SHAPERS

Where and when

- developing two-part singing in music;
- as part of learning about another culture.

Getting started

This Ghanaian song is simple but has many musical layers. Listen to the song (AP17) to see if anyone can notice a pattern in the way the melody is structured. (Each phrase starts higher than the last and the last phrase is the same as the first.) Join in with the song remembering the structure of the melody. Help everyone to feel the steady beat of the song by walking on the spot

Moving on

Perform the song as a round (AP18). Divide the class into four groups. Group 1 starts the song. When they have sung the first phrase, they continue and Group 2 starts. This sequence is repeated until each group has started.

Outcomes

- making a clear differentiation between 'n' and 'm' consonants using the sounds of another language;
- pitch-matching to a seven-note melody;
- singing a round.

TEACHING TIPS
This song needs a strong African feel. Encourage the children to find this tone of voice by asking them to call (not shout) out 'Yeah Nanuma' a few times on comfortable and then higher speaking pitches.

Three two one

PATTERN: round (AS)

One, flat seven, five,
Five, flat seven, one.
I'm strumming my bass,
I'm playing my song.

*Three, two, one, now count it forwards,
One, two, three, now count it backwards,
Three, two, one, now count it forwards,
One, two, three, back to one now!

*One, two, three, let's take it higher,
Three, four, five, now count it backwards,
Five, four, three, now take it lower,
Three, two, one, back to one now!

* indicates entry point for round

LEARNING AREAS: PITCH

Where and when

- as an introduction to patterns; showing how musical patterns fit together;
- in music as an introduction to harmony (two or more melodies played together).

Getting started

Listen to the first audio performance track (AP19) and feel the steady beat. Keep the steady beat by miming a bass guitar player. Discuss the shape of the melody each time the words are numbers ('One, flat seven', 'Three, two, one' etc). Sing along and trace the shape of the melody in the air (when the numbers go from high to low so does the melody and vice-versa).

Moving on

Divide the class into three groups. Listen to the second audio performance track (AP20) to hear the song as a round. Group 1 starts the song. Group 2 starts when group 1 reaches verse 2. Group 3 starts when group 2 reaches verse 2. As each group completes the song they start it again!

Outcomes

- combining numbering with musical skills to learn about melodic shape and pattern;
- practising pitch-matching to a seven-note melody;
- learning about direction of pitch;
- learning how musical phrases fit together to make harmony in a round.

TEACHING TIPS
Do the children notice that the words follow the pattern of the music: are they clear about 'higher' and 'lower' when we talk about pitch? Help them by giving other examples of higher and lower positioning to relate to.

PATTERN: song (Stephen Chadwick)

I've got a beat box sound,
That will rock you to the ground.
  Duff chh! Du du chh! Tchhhh!
And with a mic in my face,
I can imitate a bass.
  Dumm, du dumm du dumm!
You might sometimes hear me sing,
Oh baby, doo be doo bee doo bee do wha,
But I'm mostly doing
Those crazy beat box things!
Oh yeah!

Duff chh! Du du chh!
Dumm, dum dumm
Chhhho doo doo!
Tshworrh tick-a-tick-a-tick-a
Quack quack urgh-schick
Tchhhh!

LEARNING AREAS: SOUND SHAPERS; EXPRESSION

Where and when

- as part of a performance;
- to develop confidence in the use of the voice.

Getting started

Play the biggest cymbal you have (ideally one from a drum kit) and let everyone imitate the sound with their voices ('Tchhhh!'). Pretend to be a drum kit player and gesture to 'play' the class as a cymbal. Next, play the class as the bass drum ('Dumm, du dumm du dumm!'). Divide the class into two groups and play them as a cymbal and a bass. Listen to one of the 'Beat box rock' performance tracks. Can anyone recognise any sounds (the bass and cymbal)? Listen to the second part and learn the different beat box sounds.

Moving on

Listen to the first audio performance track (AP21) and copy the different beat box sounds in the gap provided. With the longer version of the song (AP22) the children can add beat box sounds in any order fitting in with the performer on the recording. As an ultimate challenge some children can invent and improvise beat box sounds in between each verse or perform without the backing track

Outcomes

- working the voice together with the sound shapers to create the special effects of 'beat boxing';
- exploring the voice as an instrument.

communication

Hocketting
37

ENERGISER

An entertaining but vital musical skill that can be practised anywhere with two or more people. Watch the movie demo (MD10) to see how to alternate words, notes and sung words of a song while maintaining a steady beat. It requires great concentration and timing but most of all it develops a really good sense of pitch.

Listening around you
38

LEARNING AREAS: **BODY BALANCE**

As the title suggests, this activity is about understanding what we mean by listening carefully. The children start by listening to their own breathing, then gradually focus their attention and widen their awareness of other sounds around them. This is a calming activity and it supports any area of the curriculum where listening and concentrating are important.

Gobbledigook
39

LEARNING AREAS: **PITCH; SOUND SHAPERS**

A fun tongue-twister song that rehearses vowel sounds through playing with words. The song is made of nonsense words that enable children to develop their articulation and create an overall colourful splash of sound.

Chitter chatter
40

LEARNING AREAS: **PITCH; SOUND SHAPERS**

In this song the children practise the sounds 'ch', 't', 'k', 'j' and 'y', making it valuable in literacy. It is also a simple two-part round creating the feel of a crowded room of people chattering.

Rain, rain
41

LEARNING AREAS: **PITCH; EXPRESSION**

This chant is another opportunity to think about the way in which we express ourselves with different tones of voice. The chant tells the story of a family stuck indoors because of the rain and the children are bored. Discuss with the class what makes a bored voice and what makes an excited voice. The chant also raises questions in PSHE about what we do for hobbies and can be a useful lever into history; what would children have been doing in past times – did they get as bored?

The next train to Crewe
42

LEARNING AREAS: **PITCH; EXPRESSION**

Familiarity with formal announcements is key to our communication system. This chanted round contrasts the formality of the train announcements on a public loud speaker system with phrases heard in a train station (station master, farewells etc). The children can use the chant in drama and literacy to consider who might be on the train and why.

Goodbye song
43

LEARNING AREAS: **BREATH; PITCH**

An upbeat song that uses a whole range of ways of saying goodbye depending on relationships, status and feelings. Challenge the class to find out how to say goodbye in as many languages as possible and talk about how they say goodbye to different people, such as family members and friends. Saying goodbye can evoke real feelings of insecurity and worry about endings or unknown beginnings and this is a lovely song through which such feelings can be addressed.

Clever Nan
44

LEARNING AREAS: **BREATH; PITCH; SOUND SHAPERS**

There is a range of communication methods open to everyone today and this song features the main ones in its chorus. However, it has a lovely twist in that the subject of the song may well be better off simply popping next door and talking face to face! The song affords a good opportunity to think about the history of communication and the future of communication in ICT or simply makes a very entertaining song!

I've got the news
45

LEARNING AREAS: **PITCH; SOUND SHAPERS; EXPRESSION**

Accessing the amazing feats and achievements from all round the world is the theme of this song. It is fast, upbeat and funky as are the digital data streams it talks about. The news stories are a good feature of PSHE in considering aspirations and personal achievements but the song is also a great way into discussing and creating a school news stream.

COMMUNICATION: warm up game-chant (traditional)

Where and when

- as a playground game for pairs or small groups of children;
- to help learn the melody of a song.

Getting started

Hocketting is a fun activity in which a melody is passed between two or more people/ groups. Watch the movie demo (MD10) to familiarise the children with the activity. There are three ways to hocket:

1. alternate singing the notes of the melody;
2. alternate saying the words of the song;
3. alternate singing the words of the song.

   Lead this activity with any of the three steps shown in the movie demo (words, notes, sung words): you say/sing the first note/word, and the children respond with the second, and so on.

Moving on

Divide the children into pairs or groups to hocket 'Twinkle twinkle little star'. Can the children think of other songs they all know to play the hocketting game?

Outcomes

- responding to a cue;
- improving listening and anticipation skills.

TEACHING TIPS
There will be lots of 'mistakes' when you first try out this activity, so make it fun!

Listening around you

MD2 ?

LEARNING AREAS: BODY BALANCE

Where and when

- when preparing the class to focus and listen to instructions for completing a new task;
- as part of a drama lesson; everyone listens to identified sounds around them and responds accordingly;
- when exploring the five human senses: sight, sound, taste, touch and smell.

Getting started

Singing well is also about listening: watch the movie demo and ask the children what they noticed about the different ways of listening? (Inside, outside, near, far.)

Moving on

Everyone participates in the activity shown on the movie demo. Guide the children with these instructions: 1) put your hands over your ears and listen to your own breathing; 2) breathe as quietly as you can, so that you can't hear any extra noises in your ears; 3) drop your hands and listen out for your neighbours' breathing; 4) listen to the other sounds in the room (you can mention examples of sounds that they will be able to hear); 5) listen to the sounds outside the room (you can mention sounds that they will be able to hear).

Outcomes

- developing listening, focusing and awareness skills.

Gobbledigook

COMMUNICATION: nonsense song (Barry Gibson)

Gobbledigook, gobbledigook,
Properly poppily, loppily loop,
Hoppily boppily, sloppily soup,
Gobbledi~ gobbledi~ gook.

Bubbly gum, bubbly gum,
Mumbly bumbly, rumbly tum,
Rubbly doubly, jumbly jum,
Bubbly, bubbly gum.

Diggety jig, diggety jig,
Quickety pickety, flickety flick,
Hickory dickory, tickety tick,
Diggety, diggety jig.

LEARNING AREAS: PITCH; SOUND SHAPERS

Where and when

- in literacy to practise vowel sounds.

Getting started

This is a nonsense song full of words that don't mean anything. Listen to the song; the first and the last lines of each verse are the same. Each verse starts on a higher note. Divide the class into three groups and allocate a verse to each group with everyone in the class joining in on the first and last lines. Sing along with the audio track; can each group anticipate its new start note?

Moving on

Divide the children into small groups to invent their own new nonsense verses. Can they sing them to the rest of the class?

Outcomes

- practising pitch-matching to a four-note melody that changes start note;
- working the sound shapers with multiple consonant onsets to improve articulation;
- combining language and vocal skills in a nonsense tongue twister.

TEACHING TIPS
We need lips, tongue and teeth as well as breath to make clear plosive sounds such as 'g', 'p', 't' and 'b'. Help the children find the energy needed to perform this song well by getting them to say 'gobbledigook' slowly and clearly, then increasing the speed.

Chitter chatter

COMMUNICATION: round (Barry Gibson)

Chitter chatter, chitter chatter,
*Yak yak yak,
Chitter chatter, chitter chatter,
Talk right back.

Chitter chatter, chitter chatter
Jaw jaw jaw,
Chitter chatter, chitter chatter,
Talk some more.

(repeat once)

* indicates entry point for round

LEARNING AREAS: PITCH; SOUND SHAPERS

Where and when

- when beginning to sing in two different parts;
- to practise phonics.

Getting started

Listen to the first audio performance track (AP24). When the children are familiar with the song, join in. Can the children identify the repeated sounds and words in the lyrics? ('Chitter chatter', 'yak', 'jaw'.) Practise saying these sounds clearly.

Moving on

Discuss where we find lots of people talking (parties, markets, coffee shops). To help create the effect of talking, sing the song in two parts. First, listen to the second audio performance track (AP25). Then divide the class into two groups to sing it as a round.

Outcomes

- practising pitch-matching with repeated notes, small and large steps in an four-note melody;
- improving articulation by working the sound shapers on 'ch', 't', 'k', 'j' and 'y';
- learning to sing a round.

TEACHING TIPS

Rounds are an excellent way for us to learn about part-singing. Some children may be put off their part of the tune when they hear others singing a different part. This is quite normal. You can help by getting the children to sing in small groups and also separating them into corners of the classroom. When they are confident with their 'parts' ask the groups to walk towards each other while they are still singing.

Rain, rain

COMMUNICATION: chant (AS)

Rain, rain,
Rain all morning,
I'm stuck inside,
And it's really, really, really boring.

Rain, rain,
Rain all morning,
I'm stuck inside
And the news is on the telly,
  'Blah blah blah, blah blah blah',
And it's really, really, really boring.

Rain, rain,
Rain all morning,
I'm stuck inside and my
Little sister's whining,
  'Why? Why?',
And the news is on the telly,
  'Blah blah blah, blah blah blah',
And it's really, really, really boring.

Rain, rain,
Rain all morning,
I'm stuck inside and my
Mum's too busy,
  'Just a minute', 'just a minute',
And my little sister's whining,
  'Why? Why?'
And the news is on the telly,
  'Blah blah blah, blah blah blah',
And it's really, really, really boring.

Rain, rain,
Rain all morning,
I'm stuck inside,
And the door bell rings,
  'Dring dring, dring dring',
And my friend Jack says,
  'Cheer up! Look!
  The rain's stopped!'

LEARNING AREAS: PITCH; EXPRESSION

Where and when

- in PSHE when considering hobbies and free time;
- in history when learning about the place of children in society over time.

Getting started

Listen to the audio demo (AD4). Ask the children how many characters there are in the story. What sort of mood is each character in and how can we tell?

Moving on

Listen to the chant and join in with: the newsreader's 'Blah, blah, blah', the little sister's 'Why? Why?', the mother's 'Just a minute' and the doorbell 'Dring dring'. Make the differences between the sounds very clear. Perform the whole chant as a class either with everyone together or with soloists on the newsreader, little sister and Mum's part. Make sure that the narrator's voice always sounds very bored. Jack should be a bright contrast!

Outcomes

- improving auditory awareness of tone of voice and change of pitch in speech;
- exploring using specific tones of voice for expressive purposes.

TEACHING TIPS
Tone of voice and pitch give important signals in speaking voice. Encourage the children to make clear differences between the bored voice of the narrator and the newsreader, the whining voice of little sister, the mother's calling voice and Jack's cheerful voice at the end.

The next train to crewe

The next train to Crewe will depart from
  Platform Two,
*Chuff chuff whoooo! Chuff chuff whoooo!
The next train to Crewe will depart from
  Platform Two,
Chuff chuff whoooo! Chuff chuff whoooo!

Bye bye, I'll be back soon,
All aboard! All aboard!
Bye bye, I'll be back soon,
All aboard! All aboard!

* indicates entry point for round

LEARNING AREAS: PITCH; EXPRESSION

Where and when

- in a drama session: who is on the train and why?
- on a school journey.

Getting started

Listen to the first audio demo (AD5). Explore the difference between the platform announcement voice and the 'All aboard' voice. (One is level, clear, and very factual and using a speaking voice as they have a tannoy system to carry their voice; the other is calling out, warning us the train will leave, it has no microphone and the person must raise the volume of their voice.) Focus on the 'Chuff chuff whoooo!' sound and 'Bye bye, I'll be back soon'. What do the children notice about the pitch of these chants? ('Chuff chuff' is low, 'whoooo!' is high; 'Bye bye' starts high and moves lower.)

Moving on

Listen to the first audio demo (AD5) and learn the chant. When the children are very familiar with it, listen to the second audio demo (AD6) which demonstrates how the chant works as a round. Divide the children into two groups to perform the round.

Outcomes

- developing listening skills;
- gaining awareness of emotions in tone of voice;
- combining rhythmic patterns in a round.

Goodbye song

COMMUNICATION: song (Ana Sanderson and Matthew White)

You can go by boat,
Go by train,
Or walk upon your feet.
You can go by car,
Go by plane,
Or dance along the street.

Bon voyage, catch ya later,
Toodle-oo, gotta fly.
It doesn't matter how you say it,
The meaning is still goodbye.
Au revoir, gonna miss ya,
Keep in touch, it's been swell.
It doesn't matter how you say it,
The meaning is still farewell.

You can take a cab,
Take a hike,
Or float in a balloon.
You can take a bus,
Take a bike,
Or rocket to the moon.

Bon voyage, catch ya later,
Toodle-oo, gotta fly.
It doesn't matter how you say it,
The meaning is still goodbye.
Au revoir, gonna miss ya,
Keep in touch, it's been swell.
It doesn't matter how you say it,
The meaning is still farewell.

LEARNING AREAS: BREATH; PITCH

Where and when
- in PSHE when talking about saying goodbye;
- as a leaving song.

Getting started
Find examples of how to say goodbye in as many languages as possible. As a group discuss any examples of having to say goodbye and how the individuals felt: were they really glad to say goodbye, or perhaps upset to say farewell? Listen to the song and discuss how many different ways of saying goodbye are mentioned in the song. Join in the chorus, adding some goodbye actions (eg waving, a thumbs up, shrugging the shoulders, pretending to write on a note pad, putting a phone down etc). The second half of the chorus is the same as the first.

Moving on
This song contains a mixture of short and longer phrases. The movie demo will help the children manage the different phrase lengths. Watch the movie demo and encourage the children to put their hands on their tummies like the singer in the movie while they sing the song.

Outcomes
- pitch-matching to an eight-note melody;
- gaining conscious control of breathing for short and long phrases.

Clever Nan

COMMUNICATION: song (David Sheppard)

Struggling with my homework,
Don't know what to do,
So many problems I can't solve,
I haven't got a clue.
Then I had my big idea,
Formed my masterplan,
It's obvious the thing to do,
I'll ask my clever Nan.

Phoning, texting, sending emails,
Still not getting through.
Come on Nan, do me a favour,
Got to speak to you.
All my new technology,
It seems a shame to waste,
But I think I'll have to pop next door,
And ask her face to face.

Trained my carrier pigeon,
To land right on her porch,
Tried to send a message,
Using morse code with my torch.
I'd shout down through the window,
But that would seem so wrong,
When Nan's got a lovely mobile phone,
I wish she'd turn it on.

Phoning, texting, sending emails,
Still not getting through.
Come on Nan, do me a favour,
Got to speak to you.
All my new technology,
It seems a shame to waste,
But I think I'll have to pop next door,
And ask her face to face.

LEARNING AREAS: PITCH; SOUND SHAPERS; EXPRESSION

When and where

- in ICT when discussing appropriate ways of communicating;
- in an end of year performance.

Getting started

This is a humorous song about using lots of different types of communication (that ultimately fail) when really it would have been more appropriate to speak to a person face to face in the first place! Learn the chorus first by joining in. Simple actions may help (eg pretending to use the range of communications). Then add the verses.

Moving on

Ask the children to decide what it was the person in the song wanted to ask Nan about and write it as an email, a letter and a text message. Discuss the differences between these forms of communication. How else can we communicate (sign language, stories, newspaper articles)? How does the class think we may be communicating one hundred years from now?

Outcomes

- practising pitch-matching to a seven-note melody;
- learning to deliver lots of words and ideas within a song.

I've got the news

COMMUNICATION: song (Matthew Holmes)

News reporter: **Live around the world, from Studio 9, this is the news, good evening.**

There's a girl in an aeroplane,
Coming to you live, about to do a sky dive.
She cuts the air like a hurricane,
Watch her as she flies,
She's soaring from the bright skies.
That was amazing,
Show me all the views,
This is not a movie,
This is the news!

On my video, audio, digital data stream,
From the internet to my mobile phone,
I've got the news if you know what I mean.

News reporter: **Let's cross live!**

There's a boy on Mount Everest
Climbing to the top,
So young and yet he won't stop.
He's right up there with the very best,
Think he's nearly there,
Let's radio a fanfare.
That was amazing!
Pictures we can use,
Satellites are calling,
This is the news!

On my video, audio, digital data stream...

News reporter: **And now, the sports news!**

There's a striker who's super fast,
Wow! He's just a teen,
A blur across the small screen.
Defenders diving, he's flying past,
Ev'ry time he scores,
The crowds are in an uproar.
That was amazing!
Grab some interviews,
All around the planet,
This is the news!

On my video, audio, digital data stream... (x2)

LEARNING AREAS: PITCH; EXPRESSION

When and where

- in PSHE about aspirations and believing in yourself;
- in literacy, when planning a newspaper front page.

Getting started

Scour newspapers and consider amazing news events that involve children locally or nationally. What amazing things do the members of the class want to do or have already done that would make the news headline? Create a news stream of events in your lives and a front page for a school newspaper.

Moving on

Listen to the recording and get a feel for the style and the steady beat of the song. Join in the chorus and then the 'That was amazing!' sections. When everyone is confident learn, the rest of the verses. Invite individuals to perform to the backing track, karaoke-style. Alternatively divide the children into groups: newsreaders, reporters and news watchers.

Outcomes

- gaining conscious control when pitch-matching to a seven-note melody;
- moving from a spoken voice to a singing voice;
- making a dramatic scene from song material.

 Movement

Alphabet rhyme
47

ENERGISER

A rhythmic alphabet chant which plays with words based on the sequence of the letters of the alphabet. The chant is performed by two groups whose lines overlap and is even more fun with actions added to match the lyrics.

Moveability
48

LEARNING AREAS: **BODY BALANCE**

A physical and vocal warm up based on movements inspired by the ancient Chinese tradition of Chi Gung. Watch the movie performance to learn the moves of each verse and enjoy the simple, repetitive lyrics which capture the quality of each movement.

Makarona
49

LEARNING AREAS: **BREATH; SOUND SHAPERS**

This traditional Polish children's game song is usually played in pairs as a competitive clapping game. The song has nonsense words and a strong beat to clap. Invite the children to devise new clapping patterns in pairs or groups.

Let's go zudie-o
50

LEARNING AREAS: **BODY BALANCE; PITCH**

'Let's go zudie-o' is the Afro-American version of a well-known dance song which has many variations around the world. In this version an individual child contributes ideas for actions for everyone to copy.

Supersonic
51

LEARNING AREAS: **PITCH; EXPRESSION**

A short rock-style song which is sung on progressively higher starting notes, creating a musical climax as part of the preparation for a race. It is great for extending the children's pitch range and can also be sung as a round.

Cricket carnival
52

LEARNING AREAS: **BODY BALANCE; PITCH**

A joyful calypso with dance actions to perform as you sing. The theme of minibeasts and their characteristic movements can be combined with work in science or developed into a carnival performance.

Ignition lightspeed
53

LEARNING AREAS: **PITCH; EXPRESSION**

The subject of this song is space exploration and it incorporates a lot of scientific vocabulary as well as a countdown to lift off! The chorus is sung in two overlapping groups and provides a good introduction to part-singing.

Voices calling
54

LEARNING AREAS: **BREATH; PITCH; EXPRESSION**

This song has a haunting, lyrical melody and its subject is animal migration and the environmental issues of survival. There are several different sections for the children to learn and perform in groups to build a large performance for assembly or a concert.

Alphabet rhyme

MOVEMENT: chant (AS)

Group 1: **A, B, C,**

    Group 2: **See, there's a puppet on a string,**

Group 1: **D, E, F,**

    Group 2: **Effortlessly doing its thing,**

Group 1: **G, H, I,**

    Group 2: **I don't need strings to move in time,**

All: (clap clap) **Listen to the alphabet rhyme.**

Group 1: **J, K, L,**

    Group 2: **Elephants can swing and sway,**

Group 1: **M, N, O,**

    Group 2: **Ogres frighten children away,**

Group 1: **P, Q, R,**

    Group 2: **Armies just keep marching in time,**

All: (clap clap) **Listen to the alphabet rhyme.**

Group 1: **S, T, U,**

    Group 2: **You are you and I am me,**

Group 1: **V, W, X,**

    Group 2: **Excellent, together we'll be,**

Group 1: **Y, Z,**

    Group 2: **A team.**

All: **Now chant in time...**

(clap clap) **Listen to the alphabet rhyme!**

(clap clap) **Listen to the alphabet rhyme!**

(clap clap) **Listen to the alphabet rhyme!**

Yeah!

ENERGISER

Where and when

- in literacy/phonics work;
- as preparation for two-part singing.

Getting started

Listen to the audio demo (AD7). Join in with chanting the alphabet. When the chant is more familiar, join in with the fourth line of each verse: '(clap clap) Listen to the alphabet rhyme'.

Moving on

Make up actions to go with the second part of the rhyme (eg 'See, there's a puppet on a string'). When the whole chant is familiar, divide the children into two groups: the alphabet group and the rhyme group. Notice that the group 1 third letter is the same as the group 2 first syllable and that they coincide. Perform this two-part chant with actions. Everyone can strike a pose at the end – puppet/ogre/elephant, etc.

Outcomes

- combining rhythmic, physical and language skills;
- learning to anticipate when to start chanting;
- feeling energised and co-ordinated.

moveability

MOVEMENT: song (words by Barry Gibson/Jeremy Fisher, music by Barry Gibson)

Move, move, moveability,
Move, move, moveability,
Move, move, moveability,
Moveability now!

Chop, chop, chopability,
Chop, chop, chopability,
Chop, chop, chopability,
Chopability now!

Squeeze, squeeze, squeezability...

Stretch, stretch, stretchability...

Push, push, pushability...

Fan, fan, fanability...

Bounce, bounce, bounceability...

Ski, ski, skiability...

Move, move, moveability...

LEARNING AREAS: BODY BALANCE

Where and when

- at any time when the children need a physical activity break;
- as a fun warm up before singing, PE or dance.

Getting started

This is a song with a sequence of specific movements inspired by the ancient Chinese tradition of Chi Gung. Watch the movie performance and join in with the movements.

Moving on

When the children are very familiar with the movements and their sequence, ask them to join in with the song.

Outcomes

- feeling balanced, focused and ready to sing;
- improving physical co-ordination.

TEACHING TIPS
Make sure that you and the children copy the moves on the movie performance as accurately as possible to enjoy this ancient Chinese form more fully.

Makarona

MOVEMENT: clapping game (traditional Polish)

O mone, mone, mone,
Makarona cziku daj,
Cziku daj, daj, daj, cziku daj.

O leppe, leppe, leppe,
In de kleppe in de haus,
In de haus, haus, haus, in de haus.

(repeat twice)

LEARNING AREAS: BREATH; SOUND SHAPERS

Where and when

- learning about children's games from other cultures;
- in PSHE as a paired activity.

Getting started

Play the audio performance track to the children and ask them to keep the beat as they listen, alternating hand claps with tapping both hands on the knees. Ask the children to stand in pairs, facing their partner and clap the beat as you listen again. This time, alternate one clap with your own hands together, then clap your partner's hands.

Moving on

Learn the song, then divide the children into two circles, one inside the other, so that each child has a partner from the other circle. Perform the song unaccompanied, with the hand clapping patterns. At the end of one verse, the inner circle moves one place clockwise and the children repeat the song with new partners. Continue this until the children have played with several new partners. You may also like the children to work in pairs and invent their own clapping patterns for the song.

Outcomes

- working the sound shapers using the sounds of other languages;
- practising finding space for the in-breath.

TEACHING TIPS
This is an example of a song in which there are small spaces for the in-breath (MD4). Use this as a song to monitor children's progress in breathing. Who seems to be running out of breath? Does anyone have a 'reversed breathing pattern' (see MD5)?

Let's go zudie-o

MOVEMENT: playground game (traditional Afro-American)

Let's go zudie-o, zudie-o, zudie-o
Let's go zudie-o all night long.
We're walking through the alley, alley, alley,
We're walking through the alley all night long.

Step back, Sally, Sally, Sally,
Step back, Sally all night long.
And here comes another one, 'nother one,
  'nother one.
Here comes another one all night long.

Let's go zudie-o, zudie-o, zudie-o...
We're jumping through the alley...

Step back, Meezak, Meezak, Meezak...

Let's go zudie-o, zudie-o, zudie-o...
We're skipping through the alley...

Step back, Anthony, Anthony, Anthony...

Let's go zudie-o, zudie-o, zudie-o...
We're rolling through the alley...

Step back, Joe, Joe, Joe,
Step back, Joe all night long.

LEARNING AREAS: BODY BALANCE; PITCH

Where and when

- in a dance lesson;
- at an evening dance celebration event.

Getting started

This Afro-American playground game can also be found in different variations in Britain's folk heritage ('Here's comes Barnaby'). It is a good game for developing a sense of pulse and creating physical movements to the beat.

Learn the song first then stand in two facing lines. As you sing the chorus ('Let's go zudie-o... all night long'), the named child at the end of the line (eg Sally) performs the appropriate movement to the beat, walking up and down between the lines as everyone sings and claps. At 'Step back', she goes to join the end of the line and a second child from the top of the line on the opposite side comes out to repeat the game.

Moving on

Play the singing game unaccompanied, using the children's own suggestions for movements, eg swimming, flying, turning, creeping or boogying!

Outcomes

- practising pitch-matching to a four-note melody;
- combining rhythmic, physical and singing skills.

supersonic

MOVEMENT: round (AS)

See I'm supersonic,
My *body is bionic,
I've *powers astronomic,
I can *win this race!

(repeat twice)

indicates entry point for round

LEARNING AREAS: PITCH; EXPRESSION

Where and when

- at the start of a PE lesson, alternating with physical warm ups, eg bending and stretching.

Getting started

Discuss what happens on a athletics track at the 'Get, ready, set, go' signals at the beginning of a running race. Discuss the three body positions that runners use, and let the children try these out.

Listen to the first audio performance (AP32). Ask the children what they notice about the pitch shape of the melody (it has repeating patterns which gradually rise in pitch; some notes stay on the same pitch; there is a large jump down in pitch at the end.) Can the children link the pitch shape with the start positions of a race? Build up the phrases until the children can sing the whole song. Punch the air as you sing the last phrase to give energy and win the race!

Moving on

Listen to the second audio performance (AP33) to hear 'Supersonic' performed as a round. Divide the children into two, three or four groups to sing it as a round.

Outcomes

practising pitch matching to a seven note melody;

- exploring vocal range through repeating a melody with upward steps;
- using excitement to help with finding the highest note in the song;
- learning about part-singing through singing a round.

TEACHING TIPS
Singing the same small pattern on progressively higher notes is an excellent way to extend your vocal range. You can help the children feel in control of their pitch range by using stepped hand movements on the words 'see', 'body', 'power' and 'win' (see movie demo).

cricket carnival

Crickets are grooving,
Wings are moving,
Crickets gyrating,
Legs vibrating,
Dancing's essential,
At the coolest cricket carnival.

   Hop to the left,
   Hop, hop,
   Skip to the right,
   Skip, skip,
   Jump straight ahead,
   Jump, jump,
   Come, don't be lazy,
   Let's all go crazy!
   Hop, skip and jump!
   Hop, skip and jump! Hey!

Crickets are grooving...

   Clap to the left,
   Clap, clap,
   Tap to the right,
   Tap, tap,
   Pat on your head,
   Pat, pat,
   Come don't be lazy,
   Let's all go crazy!
   Clap, tap and pat!
   Clap, tap and pat! Hey!

Crickets are grooving...

   Stamp to the left,
   Stamp, stamp,
   Bend to the right,
   Bend, bend,
   Stretch up and down,
   Stretch, stretch,
   Come, don't be lazy,
   Let's all go crazy!
   Stamp, bend and stretch!
   Stamp, bend and stretch! Hey!

Crickets are grooving...

AP34 AB41

LEARNING AREAS: BODY BALANCE; PITCH

Where and when

- in a dance lesson;
- as part of a cross-curricular project, eg on carnivals, minibeasts etc.

Getting started

Teach the children the 'Cricket carnival' dance actions, ensuring that they have space to stand and move to the left and right. Play the audio track and join in with the actions, following the instructions in the song. Gradually join in with the singing for these action verses, noticing the small upward pitch steps in the lines 'Come, don't be lazy, Let's all go crazy!'

Moving on

Teach the chorus, carefully learning the syncopated (off-beat) calypso-style rhythms. Perform the whole song with the dance actions.

Outcomes

- practising pitch-matching to a nine-note melody;
- working with small steps between notes in a rising sequence;
- improving rhythmic skills with changing rhythmic patterns;
- co-ordinating rhythm and movement.

TEACHING TIPS
Use this song to observe children's ability to co-ordinate body movements with music and rhythm: which children seem to be finding the beat easily, which need help? Which children are enjoying being creative with their dance moves; does anyone seem inhibited and shy?

Ignition lightspeed

MOVEMENT: song (Ben Glasstone)

Take flight on a jet-black night,
In a rocket to the stars,
Get ready to zoom, straight past the moon,
And take a left turn after Mars.
As the engines burn and the planets turn,
And the light years slip away,
We'll be heading out to a purple cloud,
At the heart of the Milky Way!

(Ten!) Prepare to fly my friend,
(Nine!) Way on through space and time,
(Eight!) Time to accelerate,
Across the heavens, there goes seven,
Wave goodbye to six and five,
Let's hope we make it back alive,
Four, three, two, one,
World here we come,
Ignition, what's your mission?

Group 1: Lightspeed Group 2: (Ignition, what's your mission?)
Group 1: That's the only right speed
    Group 2: (Ignition, what's your mission?)

(repeat once)

Who knows what you will find,
What wonders you may see?
When you take a trip, on a big spaceship,
To the edge of the galaxy.
It's a mystery zone but it could be home,
To another form of life.
And when the ship descends, we could be
    making friends,
Or fighting to survive.

(Ten!) Prepare to fly my friend...

Group 1: Lightspeed Group 2: (Ignition, what's your mission?)
Group 1: That's the only right speed
    Group 2: (Ignition, what's your mission?)

(repeat three times)

LEARNING AREAS: PITCH; EXPRESSION

Where and when
- as part of science work on space;
- in music lessons exploring different styles and genres of song.

Getting started
Listen to the song and discuss the scientific facts about space mentioned in the lyrics.

Teach the children the two repeating phrases from the song: 'Lightspeed (Ignition, what's your mission?)'. Divide into two groups to practise singing these so that they overlap. Play the audio performance to demonstrate how this works, then play the whole song again, asking the children to join in with the two repeating phrases. All join in with the countdown as it becomes familiar, displaying the lyrics if needed.

Moving on
Learn the two verses by memory or by using the lyrics as an aid until they become familiar. Divide the class into two groups to perform the countdown section – one group singing the phrases sung by the solo voice, the other performing the number phrases.

Practise performing the whole song, singing the verses in unison then dividing into two groups.

Outcomes
- pitch-matching to a six-note melody;
- improving recognition of melodic pattern;
- contrasting the spoken voice and the singing voice for expressive purposes;
- singing a chorus in two parts.

voices calling

MOVEMENT: song (Stephen Chadwick)

AP36 AB43   MD9 ?

All:

Voices calling,
Over land and sea,
Urging you to follow
Your destiny.
Journey homeward,
Find your place of birth,
Many miles to travel
Across the Earth.

Verse 1 (Group 1):

Walking and walking
Across the vast plain,
Walking and walking
In sun, wind and rain.

All:

It's a struggle to survive,
But you've got to stay alive,
Many dangers will await,
And no one knows your fate.

Verse 2 (Group 2):

Swim and swim and swim, (x3)
Fight against the tide.
Swim and swim and swim, (x3)
Cross the ocean wide.

All: It's a struggle...

Verse 3 (Group 3):

Fly, fly, fly up high,
Fly, fly, fly on by.

All: It's a struggle...

Voices calling...

(groups 1-3 sing verses 1, 2 and 3 together)

It's a struggle...

Voices calling.

LEARNING AREAS: BREATH; PITCH; EXPRESSION

Where and when

- as part of science study into animal life cycles and migration;
- in PSHE when discussing personal determination.

Getting started

Relate this to their scientific knowledge of migration. Can they identify creatures they know about which are relevant to each verse (eg wildebeest, turtles and swallows)? Teach the chorus of the song ('Voices calling...') and sing this with the audio track.

Moving on

Learn each of the three verses. Notice that in each of the verses the words move at different speeds, verse 1 plodding, verse 2 energised and verse 3 soaring.

When the children are confident with all three verses, divide into three groups to sing them at the same time. You may like to refer to the movie demo to help the children gain confidence and skill in holding their parts.

Outcomes

- exploring contrasting tones of voice for expression;
- learning to layer musical patterns in a performance song;
- pitch-matching to an eight-note melody;
- developing breathing skills with short and longer phrases.

TEACHING TIPS
The phrase 'Fly, fly, fly up high' calls for a more extended out-breath. Raising the arms while keeping a good body balance can help with taking a bigger breath: ask the children to breathe into their middles and at the same time slowly raise their arms as they sing the phrase.

Singing Express 4 © 2011 A&C Black Publishers Ltd   54   www.singingexpress.co.uk

people

Me, Tarzan, you, Jane! 56
ENERGISER
Watch the movie performance to learn the actions for this energetic, nonsense song about Tarzan. The melodies of the verse and chorus are very similar and both sections can be sung by two groups simultaneously to make a partner song.

Jobberman 57
LEARNING AREAS: **BODY BALANCE; BREATH; SOUND SHAPERS**
Learn to chant and sing this traditional children's song from Sierra Leone in an authentic style with local dialect and movement. There is a call and response section which can help develop singing leaders. A great example of a song to sing when discussing other cultures in citizenship or geography.

Doing something 58
LEARNING AREAS: **PITCH; SOUND SHAPERS**
A gentle, simple song to sing along with a friend to share making up nonsense word patterns. Use it to encourage the children to work in pairs or small groups. Listen to the audio performance and join in with the whistling pattern too!

Mr Whatnot 59
LEARNING AREAS: **PITCH; SOUND SHAPERS; EXPRESSION**
This song contains lyrics with lots of quirky word play using questions and words which begin with 'wh'! Combine it with phonics or literacy teaching or discuss the character of Mr Whatnot of the song title.

We are the hungry children 60
LEARNING AREAS: **PITCH; EXPRESSION**
This is a thought-provoking and poignant song which reflects on poverty and famine around the world. To sing it expressively requires control of volume and there is a movie demo to help the children develop this skill. This song would make an excellent choice for an assembly on human rights.

Amazing Egyptians 61
LEARNING AREAS: **BODY BALANCE; PITCH; SOUND SHAPERS**
A large-scale performance song which describes many different aspects of Ancient Egyptian culture and beliefs. Research Ancient Egyptian art in history book or using the internet to find inspiration for dance moves to add to the song.

Me, Tarzan, you, Jane!

PEOPLE: round (author unknown)

Me, Tarzan, you, Jane!
Flying through the air like an aeroplane!
When I fall now and again, I feel pain!
Argh! Yeah, yeah, yeah!

*Shoo-bi-doo-bi, shoo-bi-doo-bi,
   shoo-bi do waa-waa!
Shoo-bi-doo-bi, shoo-bi-doo-bi,
   shoo-bi do waa-waa!
Shoo-bi-doo-bi, shoo-bi-doo-bi,
   shoo-bi do waa-waa!
Yeah, yeah, yeah!

(repeat)

* indicates entry point for round

ENERGISER

Where and when

- as a warm up for a singing session;
- as an introduction to singing in two groups.

Getting started

Find a space where the children can perform movements freely, on the spot. Watch the movie performance to learn this humorous action song. Replay the movie performance, all joining in with the actions as you listen. Use the audio track (AP37) to practise singing each section with the rhythmical movements until everyone is confident with the song.

Moving on

When the children are confident with the song, divide into two groups to perform one section each, both at the same time. Listen to the second audio performance (AP38). Notice how the melody for each section has the same pitch shape, with different rhythms for the two sets of words. When you are ready, sing the round and invent your own moves for the second section.

Outcomes

- improving physical co-ordination through fun, rhythmic movements;
- gaining control of range with different start notes;
- singing a simple melody in two groups.

TEACHING TIPS
Make sure that the children can keep time confidently as they perform the song unaccompanied before attempting to sing in two groups. The physical movements will help them to feel the beat of the song.

Jobberman

PEOPLE: chant-song (traditional Sierra Leonean)

All chant:

Jobberman house catch-a fire,
Jobberman run away,
He went to the river to fetch some water
To help the fire down dead,
Ask a lady,
Shoo, shoo, shoo,
Ask a lady,
Shoo, shoo, shoo,
And she bend down, bend down,
And she bend down, bend down,
And she bend down, bend down,
And she bended the old man,

Shoo shoo shoo, shoo shoo, (x4)

Group 1 sing: **Ah moh seena day a-oh,** Group 2 chant: **OH!** (x4)

All chant: **Shoo shoo shoo, shoo shoo,** (x4)

Group 1 chant: **Amilo!** Group 2 chant: **Amiloma!** (x4)

Group 1: **Amiloma!** Group 2: **Amilo!** (x4)

All chant: **Shoo shoo shoo, shoo shoo.** (x4)

LEARNING AREAS: BODY BALANCE; BREATH; SOUND SHAPERS

Where and when

- in geography work on contrasting environments and cultures;
- as a performance at an international evening.

Getting started

This Sierra Leonean chant/song features kpanlogo rhythms and energised voice use. Start with the children walking on the spot to feel the pulse of the chant. Focus on the 'Amilo!' section, which is in two parts. Teach the children the 'Amiloma!' response. Focus on the 'Shoo shoo shoo' sections. Then, keeping the beat with your feet, demonstrate the 'Shoo shoo shoo, shoo shoo' rhythm pattern four times for the class to copy (or listen to the audio to learn it together).

Moving on

Listen to the audio track, asking the children to join in with the sections they recognise. Teach the first chanted section of 'Jobberman', encouraging the children to improvise simple movements as they chant. Finally, teach the sung section ('Ah moh seena...'). Divide the children into two groups and perform the whole song with movements.

Outcomes

- working the breath with energised sounds, eg 'Shoo';
- experiencing the voice as an instrument through using the sounds and shapes of another language;
- responding to rhythmic pattern and beat with physical movements.

> **TEACHING TIPS**
> This energised chant-song allows the children to use their 'outside' voices. To do this safely they need to be physically engaged. Remind them to let their tummies move out when they want to breathe in and to pull their tummies in on the 'sh' sounds (see p4 and movie demo).

PEOPLE: song (Steve Grocott)

Every time I see you,
You're doing something, doing something,
Every time I see you,
You're doing something good.

What you gonna do? What you gonna say?
What you gonna sing? What you gonna play?
Let's bam-a-lam, show me how.
Let's bam-a-lam, then we'll take a bow.

Every time I see you,
You're doing something, doing something,
Every time I see you,
You're doing something good.

Everytime I see you...

What you gonna do?...
Let's hee-be-gee...

Every time I see you...

LEARNING AREAS: PITCH; SOUND SHAPERS

Where and when

- as part of a phonics work;
- in circle time as part of PSHE.

Getting started

'Doing something' gives the children opportunities to enjoy and create their own word play patterns. Listen to the audio track together and join in with the refrain 'doing something' as it becomes familiar. What do the children notice about the pitch-shape of this phrase? (It moves down in pitch, step by step.) Play the audio track and this time encourage the children to use their voices to join in with the repeated word patterns, eg 'bam-a-lam', 'hee-be-gee'.

Moving on

Learn the whole song and perform it with the backing track. Ask the children to suggest word patterns (vocables) for new verses, eg 'pong-a-wong', 'fizz-a-wiz' or 'hug-a-wug'.

Outcomes

- practising pitch-matching to a six-note melody that uses steps and small leaps in different directions;
- learning about rhythmic pattern through making up vocables to fit with the melody.

PEOPLE: song (Barry Gibson)

Let me introduce Mr Whatnot,
From Wherever-Next-on-Sea.
He does whatever Whatnots do,
Whenever that may be.
Somehow he's forever wondering,
Why ever he does what?
Why ever? Wherever?
However? Whatever?
Whether he wants to or not!

(repeat)

Why ever? Wherever?
However? Whatever?
Whether he wants to or not!

LEARNING AREAS: PITCH; SOUND SHAPERS; EXPRESSION

Where and when

- as part of spelling work on the phoneme 'wh-';
- in PSHE when discussing children's thoughts and questions;
- as a stimulus for creative writing about an imaginary character.

Getting started

Listen to the audio track together, asking the children to identify all the different words beginning with 'w/wh' in the song. What do the children think the character of 'Mr Whatnot' is like? (Puzzled, inquisitive, hesitant, curious, nosy, worried, intelligent.) What sort of questions do the children think he comes up with?

Moving on

Teach the whole song, noticing the jaunty rhythms and light singing style. Can the children sing it as if they are describing a slightly puzzled 'Mr Whatnot'. Can they emphasise all the words that start with a 'w'? Can they make the last line fun by shrugging their shoulders and gesturing with their hands?

Outcomes

- working with leaps and steps in a seven-note melodic pattern;
- enjoying word play as an expressive device in song;
- improving articulation through use of different words starting with the phoneme 'w'.

TEACHING TIPS
In singing, expression and phrasing are linked. Encourage the children to have fun with the words of the song and this will help them with the expressive shapes of the phrases.

we are the hungry children

PEOPLE: song (David Moses)

Do you know the way it feels to be hungry,
And you need a biscuit or a sweet?
When you think about the smell of your
   favourite food,
Do you long for something nice to eat?

   We are the hungry children, feed us,
   We are the hungry children, feed us.

Do you know the way it feels to be hungry,
And your lunch is still some time away?
What you had to eat at breakfast seems so
   long ago,
And you've only just come in from play.

   We are the hungry children...

Do you know the way it feels to be hungry,
   and your food costs more than you can pay?
All you'll get to eat today is what's left from
   yesterday, all dried up and sticking to
   your plate.

   We are the hungry children...

Do you know the way it feels to be hungry,
And your inside's empty as the air?
Just a cup of plain boiled rice has to last you
   all day,
Nothing else, there's no more left to spare.

   We are the hungry children...

Do you know the way it feels to be hungry,
When the truck bringing rice doesn't come?
There will be no food today, so there's nothing
   to do,
But to lie there crying in the sun.

   We are the hungry children...

LEARNING AREAS: PITCH; EXPRESSION

Where and when

- as part of a citizenship discussion about human rights and living in a diverse world;
- in a geography project when comparing different cultures.

Getting started

This gentle, thoughtful song raises an important human issue by relating it to the children's own experience. Listen to the song together, joining in with the chorus as it becomes familiar. Ask the children what they think the song is about and discuss the issues raised in its lyrics.

Moving on

Teach the verses one at a time, noticing the similar start to the melody of each line. Encourage the children to use their voices expressively as they ask the questions and think about the meaning and context of the words of each different verse. Notice that each verse gets louder and higher until the final verse which is quieter, lower and more thoughtful.

Outcomes

- practising pitch-matching to a five-note melody;
- gaining control of range with different start notes;
- learning to control volume (dynamics) to create a dramatic effect.

TEACHING TIPS
Watch the movie demo. Rehearse the children with the different volume levels shown. Use the hand movements to help with the control of volume (dynamics).

Amazing Egyptians

PEOPLE: song (Suzy Davies)

Amazing Egyptians,
Exciting Egyptians,
Amazing Egyptians,
Exciting Egyptians,
Ancient inscriptions,
Dramatic depictions,
From ages before us,
Now here comes the chorus:

To be amid the pyramids,
To ride in style down the Nile,
Having a rare old time with a Pharaoh,
Worshipping cats, cows, jackals and crocodiles.
Here's looking at ya, Cleopatra,
Tutankhamun come and take me back in time.

Known as a nation,
For mummification,
They wrote on papyrus,
And how they inspire us!

To be amid the pyramids...

Who was the nicest,
Osiris or Isis?
Anubis or Horus?
Now here comes the chorus:

To be amid the pyramids...

Here's looking at ya Cleopatra,
Tutankhamun come and take me back in time.
Here's looking at ya Cleopatra,
Tutankhamun come and take me back in time.

Egyptians!

LEARNING AREAS: BODY BALANCE; PITCH; SOUND SHAPERS

Where and when

- as part of a history project on the Egyptians;
- as a performance in a concert.

Getting started

Listen to the audio performance of the whole song and then discuss the words and phrases that the children noticed, relating them to their knowledge of Ancient Egypt. Ask the children for suggestions for simple dance moves that will make them look like Ancient Egyptians or actions to illustrate the lyrics of the song.

Moving on

Sing the first verse. The melody uses two notes and consists of short rhythmic phrases. Then sing the chorus. This is higher, and the third and fourth lines are longer and have more syllables to fit in. When the children can sing the song confidently, add their simple dance moves to create a performance.

Outcomes

- creating physical movements to fit the rhythm and feel of a song;
- pitch-matching to a seven-note melody; gaining recognition of different melodic patterns;
- enjoying alliteration, assonance and humour in a lively narrative.

TEACHING TIPS
Make sure that the simple dance moves are not too energetic so that the children are still able to breathe easily and sing the song effectively.

Acknowledgements

The authors and publishers would like to thank the following for their generous support and advice in the preparation of **Singing Express 4**:

Philip Ashby, Chris Bartram, James Bachmann, Em Whitfield Brooks, Stephen Chadwick, Kim Chandler, Jacqui Doughty, Christiane Engel, Jon Finnigan, Barry Gibson, Ben Glasstone, Steve Grocott, Matthew Holmes, Jason Lane, Jocelyn Lucas, Val and David Machell, Paloma Gomez Martinez, Matthew Moore, David Moses, Sue Nicholls, Nigel Pilkington, Ian Shepherd, Saffron Stocker, Kate Stonham, Anthony Strong, Doreen Thorogood, Kaye Umansky, Professor Graham F Welch, Matthew White and Kirsty Young.

All works by Ana Sanderson (AS), Gillyanne Kayes (GK), Jeremy Fisher (JF), Helen MacGregor (HM) and Maureen Hanke (MH) were written by the authors for **Singing Express 4** © administered by A&C Black Publishers.

The works by writers listed below were selected/written for **Singing Express 4** and copyright of the works is administered by A&C Black Publishers:

Stephen Chadwick for **Beat box rock**, **Cricket carnival**, **Voices calling**.

Barry Gibson for **All year round; Breathing and breezing along; Chitter chatter; Fit together; Gobbledigook; Mr Whatnot; Tumble down; Under the bridge.**

Barry Gibson for **Moveability** (music); **Barry Gibson** and **Jeremy Fisher** for **Moveability** (words).

Ben Glasstone for **Ignition lightspeed**.

Steve Grocott for **Doing something**.

Matthew Holmes for **Endangered species**; **I've got the news**.

David Moses for **Water water everywhere**.

David Sheppard for **Clever Nan**; **Global warming**.

Ana Sanderson and **Matthew White** for **Goodbye song**.

Kirsty Young for **Sound map**.

The copyright holders of the works have granted their permission for the inclusion of their works in **Singing Express 4**.

Suzy Davies for **Amazing Egyptians; What's it worth, planet Earth?**

Ian Lawrence for **Tales of long ago and far away**.

Helen MacGregor for **Red Riding Hood**

David Moses for **We are the hungry children** (this version specially adapted for Singing Express 4).

All audio and movie backings and performances were created specially for **Singing Express 4** and are copyright A&C Black Publishers. The authors and Publishers thank the following for their work:

Vocalists/Presenters: Rosemary Amoani, Neil Bett, Kim Chandler, Jeremy Fisher, Matthew Holmes, Amanda McKett, Ben Parry, Rachel Platt, Nigel Pilkington, Bridgitta Roy, Kaz Simmons, Helen Speirs, Anthony Strong, Cleveland Watkiss, Matthew White.

Live backing instrumentalists: rock kit – Jon Finnigan.

Studio backings: **James Bachmann** (Apples and bananas, Throw it out the window), **Barry Gibson** (All year round, Breathing and breezing, Chitter chatter, Fit together, Global warming, Gobbledigook, Let's go zudie-o, Mr Whatnot, Moveability, Tumble down, Under the bridge); **Ben Glasstone** (Ignition lightspeed, Makarona); **Steve Grocott** (Doing something); **Matthew Holmes** (Endangered species, I've got the news); **Chris Hussey** (What's it worth, planet Earth?); **Matthew Moore** (Joshua fit the battle of Jericho, Me, Tarzan, you, Jane!, Supersonic, Tales of long ago and far away, Water water everywhere); **David Moses** (The lemon tree, We are the hungry children).

All other studio backings including those to his own original songs were created by **Stephen Chadwick.**

All films were created especially for **Singing Express 4** by Walk Tall Media (Walk Tall Media Ltd, 9 Kennington Road, Bath, BA1 3EA 01225 460 696 or 0777 171 0705) and are the copyright of A&C Black Publishers Ltd. Location footage licensed to A&C Black Publishers is the copyright of Walk Tall Media.

Jacqui Doughty – Producer and Editor; Kate Stonham – Studio Director; Philip Ashby – Studio Camera and Editor; David Brabants – Studio Sound Recordist.

Every effort has been made to trace and acknowledge copyright holders. If any right has been omitted the Publishers offer their apologies and will rectify any error in subsequent editions following notification in writing by the copyright holder.

Other titles by A&C Black for classroom music making

Michael Rosen's Sonsense Nongs

Michael Rosen's favourite silly songs - with acrobatic actions, rappy rhymes and an orchestra of annoying noises, including *Joe's got a head like a ping-pong ball*, *Susanna's a fanciful cow* and *I'm a little wrong note*. The songs are excellent for improving both literacy and singing skills and the book comes complete with a singalong CD.

Mango Spice

A Caribbean carnival of songs - for work, love, faith and fun! This fantastic selection of 44 Caribbean songs includes fun playalong accompaniments, a wealth of background information and an up-to-date bibliography and discography, making it a superb cross-curricular Carribean music resource for 5-11 year olds.

The CD contains all the songs in the book - sung (to assist with pronunciation) and with authentic accompaniments.

Flying a Round

A lively collection of rounds and partner songs, graded in difficulty, some original and some familiar, and from all around the world, including Baby sardine, Things that go bump in the night, Junkanoo and Zum gali gali. One for every occasion! There are suggestions for accompaniment on recorder, guitar and percussion. The CD includes performances of all the songs – making this an ideal resource for both music specialists and less confident readers of music.

Kickstart Music 2

Pick up and play! Whether you want to spend 10 minutes or two hours on music, *Kickstart Music 2* is a complete activity pack for 7-9 year-olds. Bursting with inspiring music ideas, it has practical instructions for engaging lessons covering the entire subject.

Whatever your resources or previous music teaching knowledge, *Kickstart Music 2* is a step-by-step, no nonsense guide to confident, effective music teaching. The book includes guidance and activities covering all musical elements such as rhythm, composition, listening, playing and singing.

Kickstart Music 2 can be used in a variety of ways and suits holistic, flexible teaching. It is a fantastic 'dip-in' resource which practitioners can open at any page and try, but it is also a comprehensive scheme of work which can be covered from beginning to end over the course of time.

Roald Dahl's Goldilocks and the Three Bears

Roald Dahl's Goldilocks and the Three Bears is an exciting addition to A&C Black's Roald Dahl series of musicals for schools. It joins the famously infamous *Snow-White and the Seven Dwarfs* and the very smelly but loveable *Jack and the Beanstalk* in a glittering line up of wickedly funny productions which children and audiences just love.

On trial for her crimes, Goldilocks looks like the sweet little innocent who'd give us her last sweetie. Could she really be the brazen crook who stole the porridge from under the snouts of the self-respecting, harmless Bears? The Jury will decide (but who will have the last laugh?). Let the trial commence!

As with every one of these great Roald Dahl musicals, Goldilocks is based on an orchestral commission by the Roald Dahl Foundation. The concert work, from which the schools' musical is derived is by Kurt Schwertsik, and schools can use the extracts provided from the orchestral work to enhance their performances.

Other musicals available in the Roald Dahl musicals series: *Jack and the Beanstalk*, *Three Three Little Pigs*, *Little Red Riding Hood and the Wolf*, *Snow-White and the Seven Dwarfs* and *Cinderella*.

Coming soon...

Terry Pratchett's The Amazing Maurice and his Educated Rodents

Available from August 2011

Sir Terry Pratchett's ingeniously upended tale of the Pied Piper has a roving band of highly intelligent rats as its heroic protagonists. Matthew Holmes' script and songs capture the plot in a captivating musical for children to perform and everyone to enjoy.

Under the lazily, streetwise command of Maurice, a speaking cat, the rats prepare to pull their practiced scam on the town of Bad Blintz. But something's up and our heroes are scampering straight into someone else's scam – and it's not nice.

Perfect for upper primary school performances, there are parts small and large for rats – heroic, villainous and oppressed – for humans on the good side and the bad, and of course for a cat named Maurice.

The complete performance pack with its photocopiable script and piano vocal score includes everything you need for rehearsing and presenting the final show, plus there's full audio support on CD so you don't need to read a note of music.

Index of file names and track numbers

CD track	Item name	AP	AB	AD	MP	MD*
	Body circles	-	-	-	-	1 & 6
	Sound map	-	-	-	-	-
1	Breathing and breezing along	1	1	-	-	3 & 5
2	Under the bridge	2	2	-	-	-
3	Tumble down	3	3	-	-	-
4	Water water everywhere	4	4	-	-	-
5	Global warming	5	5	-	-	-
	Endangered species	-	6	1	-	-
6	What's it worth, planet Earth?	6	7	-	-	11
7	Throw it out the window	7	8	-	-	-
8	Tales of long ago and far away	8	9	-	-	4 & 5
	Jack and the beanstalk	-	10	2	-	-
	Red Riding Hood	-	11	3	-	-
9	Step back, baby	9	12	-	-	-
10	Chicka hanka	10	13	-	-	-
11	Step back, baby/Chicka hanka	11	14	-	-	9
12	The lemon tree	12	15	-	-	7
13	Joshua fit the battle of Jericho	13	16	-	-	-
	Rubber chicken	-	-	-	1	1
	The swing (moods of life)	-	-	-	-	-
14	Apples and bananas	14	17	-	-	4 & 7
15	All year round	15	18	-	-	5
16	Fit together	16	19	-	-	4
17	Nanuma	17	20	-	-	-
18	Nanuma (round)	18	21	-	-	-
19	Three two one	19	22	-	-	-
20	Three two one (round)	20	23	-	-	-
21	Beat box rock	21	24	-	-	-
22	Beat box rock (extended version)	22	25	-	-	-
	Hocketting	-	-	-	-	8 & 10
	Listening all around you	-	-	-	-	2
23	Gobbledigook	23	26	-	-	-
24	Chitter chatter	24	27	-	-	-
25	Chitter chatter (round)	25	28	-	-	-
	Rain, rain	-	29	4	-	-
	The next train to Crewe	-	30	5	-	-
	The next train to Crewe (round)	-	31	6	-	-
26	Goodbye song	26	32	-	-	4
27	Clever Nan	27	33	-	-	-
28	I've got the news	28	34	-	-	-
	Alphabet rhyme	-	35	7	-	-
29	Moveability	29	36	-	2	-
30	Makarona	30	37	-	-	4 & 5
31	Let's go zudie-o	31	38	-	-	-
32	Supersonic	32	39	-	-	8
33	Supersonic (round)	33	40	-	-	8
34	Cricket carnival	34	41	-	-	-
35	Ignition lightspeed	35	42	-	-	9
36	Voices calling	36	43	-	-	9
37	Me, Tarzan, you, Jane!	37	44	-	-	-
38	Me, Tarzan, you, Jane! (round)	38	45	-	3	-
	Jobberman	-	46	8	-	3
39	Doing something	39	47	-	-	-
40	Mr Whatnot	40	48	-	-	-
41	We are the hungry children	41	49	-	-	11
42	Amazing Egyptians	42	50	-	-	-

ABOUT THE FILE NAMES AND TRACK NUMBERS

The **Singing Express 4** DVD-ROM contains a digital copy of the book in a format suitable for display on a computer screen or whiteboard. The digital copy of each activity contains embedded audio and movie files and extra whiteboard displays accessed by clicking on the associated icon.

There are some instances in which you may wish to access the audio and movie files themselves, eg if you wish to run them in Quicktime in order to use Quicktime's AV controls (see page 6). For this reason all the audio and movie files are identified by a file name so that you can locate them easily in the DVD-ROM folders. The chart opposite lists the item names and file numbers, so for example the 'Rubber chicken' movie performance is named **MP1_RubberChicken**.

AP = audio performance track (songs)

AB = audio backing track

AD = audio demo track (chants and raps)

MP = movie performance

MD = movie demo

The track numbers (to left of item title) are for the audio performances on the audio CD.

*Movie demo titles:** Body balance: Ready position (MD1), Listening around you (MD2); Breathing: Breathing into your middle (MD3), Finding space for the in-breath (MD4), Reversed breathing (MD5), Body circles (MD6); Pitching: Finding your note – Gliding and landing (MD7), Finding your note – Stepping and jumping (MD8), Finding your note – Singing together (MD9), Hocketting (MD10); Expression: Volume control (MD11)